Praise for *Discovering the Spiritual Wisdom of Trees*

"This book speaks the language of trees. The deep wisdom of the Standing Ones is that everything belongs; nothing stands alone. Beth Norcross and Leah Rampy powerfully convey this truth as they draw on the fascinating details of forestry science, the insights of spiritual masters from various traditions, and their own intimate, lifelong experience with trees. This isn't just another 'how-to' book on spirituality. It's a passionate call to *listen* to the magnificent teachers that surround us."

—**Belden C. Lane**, PhD, author of *The Solace of Fierce Landscapes, Backpacking with the Saints*, and other books

"*Discovering the Spiritual Wisdom of Trees* by Beth Norcross and Leah Rampy is a beautiful meditation on the wisdom found in the natural world and the transformative power of being in relationship with trees. Norcross and Rampy are exceptional teachers and knowledgeable guides, graciously leading the reader down tree-lined wooded paths where they share scientific knowledge, insightful personal experience, compelling metaphors, and spiritual insights. I very much appreciated how the authors take special care to invite the reader into further exploration and integration of the themes of the book through the use of creative suggested practices. *Discovering the Spiritual Wisdom of Trees* encourages us into a more intentional balance of head and heart, being and doing, all wrapped up in a joyous celebration of the sacred presence—always available whenever we lay a grateful hand upon a sturdy trunk or expanding roots, sense the hidden potential of an unopened acorn, or take in the glory of a dappled canopy."

—**Carrie Newcomer**, Emmy-winning performer, songwriter, and recording artist: *A Great Wild Mercy* and *The Beautiful Not Yet*

"What a treasure! This book captures the extraordinary power of trees to engage humans in a reciprocal relationship that transcends words. May this valuable work, rich with scientific knowledge and spiritual insight, be widely read and enjoyed. This is a unique expression of what Thomas Berry meant by his phrase, 'The universe is a communion of subjects.'"

—**Mary Evelyn Tucker**, coauthor, *Journey of the Universe*; co-director, Yale Forum on Religion and Ecology

"The best place to look for wisdom in our climate-changing moment is to the trees. The second-best place is to Beth Norcross and Leah Rampy. Spiritually rooted, scientifically sound, and soul-filled, this book will resonate with those of us who find our spiritual home beneath the cathedral arches of a forest canopy."

—**Avery Davis Lamb**, executive director of Creation Justice Ministries

"*Discovering the Spiritual Wisdom of Trees* is a powerful reflection on nurturing a heart connection to trees by two highly educated women who discovered the limitations of the mind and the power of the heart. Beautifully written, this book will draw you deeper, energize you, and renew your soul."

—**Margaret Benefiel**, executive director of Shalem Institute; author of *Crisis Leadership* and *The Soul of a Leader*

"Trees and forests speak for all of nature. Trees opened the door to the advent of the human child. Both are connected. The tree has lived before the child, but the child cannot live without the tree. This is ancient knowledge. It is why the Celts placed their spiritual trees called *bile* into a written form called Ogham, creating the foundation of the English language in use today."

—**Diana Beresford-Kroeger**, author of *Our Green Heart*

"In *Discovering the Spiritual Wisdom of Trees*, Beth Norcross and Leah Rampy lead us on a deeply meaningful eco-spiritual journey, encouraging us to see with our hearts not only how much our earthly survival depends upon trees, but how our human lives are mirrored in their lives. We must 'crack open,' growing and adapting through struggles, and make a path to the light—a light that, despite challenges, provides hope and inspiration. Filled with stories of their own journeys and experiences, along with suggested spiritual practices, this book is a companion for those seeking greater wisdom for their own lives."

—**Rev. Susan Hendershot**, president of
Interfaith Power and Light

"I have spent many years in the presence of trees, and they are my anchor in a turbulent world. High in the craggy mountains of Nevada, you will find bristle cone pines that were seedlings when Moses was drifting down the Nile. Sit quietly within their sinews and absorb thousands of years of endurance. Beth Norcross and Leah Rampy invite each of us to sit and converse with a tree of our choice, in a park or your backyard, and draw strength from its lessons of endurance, cooperation, humility, gratitude, and hope."

—**Jonathan B. Jarvis**, 18th director of the
US National Park Service (retired)

"Beth Norcross and Leah Rampy offer a practical guide to entering into sacred conversation with a tree. There is enough of the emerging science to trust their process, but this book is grounded in the actual experience of entering into relationship with the elders who grow outside our doors. Their grounded stories and accessible invitations help the reader move past their word-based assumptions of what a tree symbolizes . . . to remembering that we really can listen with holy reverence to our arboreal kin. Trees don't just offer us metaphors to appreciate, but are bearers of profound insight for what it means to be humans in interconnected relationship with the world. This book actually does help you to discover the spiritual wisdom of trees for yourself."

—**Victoria Loorz**, author of *Church of the Wild*, founder of the Center for Wild Spirituality, and host of *The Holy Wild* podcast

"The Universe has been a spiritual reality as well as a physical reality since the beginning of time. To see every lifeform on Earth as an expression of the Divine is the wisdom we are being invited to recover, urgently, if humanity is to find healing. *Discovering the Spiritual Wisdom of Trees* witnesses with hope to the urgency of this moment."

—**John Philip Newell**, author of *The Great Search: Turning to Earth and Soul in the Quest for Healing and Home*

"As a conservationist, my best days have always been those spent in nature. The same forests that once were my childhood playground are now places where I can find solace and inspiration, and there is a spiritual element that I feel when I'm surrounded by their beauty. The authors capture this vital connection and remind us of the importance of trees to our spiritual well-being."

—**Theresa Pierno**, conservation leader

"How do we heal the rift between the human and other-than-human world, a rift that presently threatens the life of both? By seeking the wisdom of other-than-humans, among them those creatures who have made precious Earth home and habitat far longer than we. This highly personal, highly spiritual, deep and wise account by Beth Norcross and Leah Rampy will take you where your soul needs to go."

—**Larry Rasmussen**, Reinhold Niebuhr Professor Emeritus of Social Ethics, Union Theological Seminary, New York City

Discovering the Spiritual
Wisdom of Trees

Also by Leah Rampy

*Earth & Soul: Reconnecting
amid Climate Chaos*

DISCOVERING
THE SPIRITUAL
WISDOM
OF TREES

BETH NORCROSS
AND LEAH RAMPY
THE CENTER FOR SPIRITUALITY IN NATURE

Broadleaf Books
Minneapolis

29 28 27 26 25 24   1 2 3 4 5 6 7 8 9

Excerpt from Laura Martin's "What I Wish for You" used with permission.

Certain names and stories have been modified to protect the identities of
those involved.

Library of Congress Cataloging-in-Publication Data

Names: Norcross, Beth (Spiritual trainer), author. | Rampy, Leah, author.
Title: Discovering the spiritual wisdom of trees / Beth Norcross,
  Leah Rampy.
Description: Minneapolis : Broadleaf Books, 2025. | "The Center for
  Spirituality in Nature." | Includes bibliographical references and index.
Identifiers: LCCN 2024034243 (print) | LCCN 2024034244 (ebook) |
  ISBN 9798889832133 (print) | ISBN 9798889832690 (ebook)
Subjects: LCSH: Trees--Religious aspects.
Classification: LCC BL444 .N67 2025 (print) | LCC BL444 (ebook) |
  DDC 202/.12--dc23/eng/20240905
LC record available at https://lccn.loc.gov/2024034243
LC ebook record available at https://lccn.loc.gov/2024034244

Cover illustration by Kimberly Glyder
Cover design by Kimberly Glyder

Print ISBN: 979-8-8898-3213-3
eBook ISBN: 979-8-8898-3269-0

Printed in China.

Beth: For Clint, Charlie, Erin, James,
and the grandchildren—
may you always find joy and
wisdom amongst the trees

Leah: For David, Andrew, Ana,
and tree teachers everywhere

CONTENTS

CHAPTER 1

DISCOVERING OUR ROOTS

BETH AND LEAH

A walk in nature walks the soul back home.
—MARY DAVIS,
IN JOAN VORDERBRUGGEN'S *WILD CALM*

"You'll never guess where I got this tick!" Leah remarked to Beth after she spent an hour at urgent care, trying to remove the pesky forest creature from her arm. When Beth inquired as to where, Leah responded with laughter, "I was hugging a tree!"

Tree hugging has been disparaged as a kind of hippie-dippie act devoid of connection with the real environmental challenges of the world. We used to think along those lines too. We believed that the real work of conservation was a matter of employing intellect and hard work. So we earned advanced degrees, and then we got to work—in government, corporations, nonprofits, religious communities, and environmental organizations—trying to serve and "save" Earth. Beth even received an advanced degree in forestry and worked in forest policy so that she could specifically work to save the forests.

At some point, this heady approach left us longtime nature lovers worn out, burned out, and frustrated by the lack of change. Earth and the forests were in more trouble than ever.

At the same time, our spiritual lives were shifting. We both grew up in the church and continued our active involvement through adulthood. But we began to chafe when inside the four walls of the church. Our hikes in the forest became slower and more contemplative. We both discovered in the woods a deep and expansive sense of kinship and unity. Inside the church building, we felt confined, constrained, and contracted as we talked about spirituality but struggled to experience it. In the forest, we felt free, unlimited, and open to Spirit. In that sacred space, we experienced deeply and imminently the Holy Mystery moving within, around, among, and beyond all of us creatures in the holy web.

During this time, Beth sought the counsel of a wise colleague and spiritual director. She poured out what she thought was her complicated story, and her colleague listened carefully. Beth remembers saying to her, "The only place that I am sure of God's presence is when I am in the forest! What should I do?" Her spiritual director paused and offered a wry grin. Softly she said: "Well, Beth, why don't you spend more time in the woods?"

While Beth respected those who still found meaning sitting in church pews, for her, Sunday mornings became a time for walks in the forests instead. In the woods, she discovered a new and loving congregation of all beings as well as deep and meaningful ways of opening to Presence. She began leading spiritual nature walks and eventually founded the Center for Spirituality in Nature, which offers opportunities for people to develop spiritual and loving relationships with the natural world.

At the same time, Leah was finding deeper meaning in leading Earth-centered pilgrimages and retreats where all were invited to remember their connections to the living world. Her heart expanded as she accompanied pilgrims experiencing old-growth forests and led retreatants in offering blessings and gratitude to nearby woodlands. She founded the outdoor Church of the Wild Two Rivers to invite deeper awareness and sharing among human and more-than-human kin. And she poured her heart into writing a book about how we might live more deeply connected to Earth in these times on the edge of loss.

And we both fell more in love with the trees. Not only did we want to be spiritually connected to them, but we also yearned to be physically connected as well. So, yes, we started hugging trees—lots and lots of trees.

Our deepening relationship with the trees not only transformed our spiritual lives but also transformed our view toward saving Earth. First independently and then together, we realized that we are not called to *save* an Earth who is capable and wise; we are called to work alongside her, following her lead, for the well-being of all.

We came to understand that trees have a unique wisdom that can provide important inspiration, comfort, and guidance for our times—lessons in resilience, adaptation, renewal, reciprocity, and hope. With significant help from filmmaker Jane Pittman, we put together a six-week video class on the Spiritual Wisdom of Trees through which we hoped participants would find pathways to wisdom and reconnection.

The Invitation to Discover

In this book, we share some of those lessons by inviting the reader into a deep, mutual, spiritual relationship with trees. Living amid the uncertainty of climate chaos and biodiversity loss, we are experiencing loneliness, anxiety, grief, and fear. Such times call us to a fuller spiritual presence, richer connections to the world around us, and a deeper knowing that all are held within a sacred web of life.

Trees, these ancient beings whose species have graced Earth for hundreds of millions of years, have much to offer as spiritual guides and soul friends. They invite our confidence as they share knowledge gained from millennia of growth and loss. We hope this book encourages the reader to revel in the beauty and wonder of trees. We share clues from the forest for the adaptations and resilience needed for precarious times and offer encouragement from the trees for hope and renewal. And we make suggestions for living gratefully and reciprocally with our tree kin.

As we explore the wisdom trees have to offer, we'll recommend that readers find, or are found by, a particular tree teacher (or teacher tree). This tree may become a soul friend who will listen without judgment for how Spirit is at work in a reader's life. Honing our focus and deepening our connection to a particular tree allows us to grow in loving and mutual relationship with her so that we might intimately sense and absorb the spiritual wisdom she offers and understand what she might ask of us. The practice of bringing a teacher tree into your life is described in more detail in chapter 2. And we have included a suggested spiritual practice at the end of each chapter to deepen the experience with a teacher tree.

Each individual's understanding of spirituality is intensely personal and stems from relationships with their religious traditions and lived experience. While we honor all perspectives, it's important to clarify what we mean when we use the term *spiritual* since we will be using it a lot. It is our view that the Divine Source, or Spirit, that enlivens, connects, and unifies all things is present and active in the natural world, of which we humans are an important part. Everything within the cosmos is imbued with a divine or spiritual spark, apparent and available if we are open to it. Like all beings, trees carry an imprint of the holy and therefore offer a unique glimpse of how Spirit manifests among us. They illuminate for us a dimension of that sacred wholeness in which all are held. If we are open and attentive, trees offer us not only wisdom, but the opportunity for deep communion within the holy web.

Although we are approaching the forest primarily through heart and soul, we recognize the importance of ecology in helping us become more aware, understanding, and supportive of trees and their ecosystems. To this end, we offer explanations of how trees grow, feed themselves, move water, stay upright, and collaborate with others. At the same time, our experience tells us that biology is only the starting point in experiencing the fullness of who trees are and what they might offer. Integrating science and spirituality, this narrative examines wisdom held within the living world of trees and planted within each of us.

Some of the insights we share will be a source of peace, hope, and joy. Other learning will be more difficult, potentially challenging and disrupting current ways of thinking and acting.

Importantly, we remember that not all communities react to trees with the same warmth, delight, or sense of comfort that others do. In *Black Faces, White Spaces*, author Carolyn Finney offers a stark reminder that in nearly every state in the union, a tree has been and often still is "a painful symbol for many black people, reminding them that the color of their skin could mean death."[1] As we speak to spiritual connections between the trees and us, we want to remember that these relationships can be difficult and complex.

Throughout our journey with trees, perhaps the most significant thing we have discovered is the importance of opening our hearts wide if we are to absorb the wisdom the trees offer us. We invite you to discern when the time is right to be vulnerable, open fully, and completely available to whatever Holy Mystery has to offer. We acknowledge that this is not easy; it flies in the face of our cultural norms and our personal habits. Admittedly, being vulnerable did not come naturally or easily for either of us. Thankfully, trees model for us this important spiritual practice.

CHAPTER 2

CRACKING OPEN

LEAH

What is the cause of the growth of an acorn? The oak that is to come.

— JOSEPH CAMPBELL,
JOSEPH CAMPBELL FOUNDATION

Like an acorn that must crack open to become an oak, our personal journey of spiritual deepening has a lot to do with allowing our hard exteriors to soften, paying close attention to what is growing inside us and trying to break through, rooting ourselves in fertile soil, and weaving connections to the living world. This is the journey to becoming our truest selves and discovering what Buddhist nun Pema Chödrön calls our "wisdom mind."[1] Open and vulnerable, rooted and connected, we experience the Deep Knowing within each of us and all other beings. Here we sense our unity with Source, Divine Mystery.

Many significant wisdom teachers over time have shared a simple but poignant parable of a wise, scruffy acorn to illustrate the challenges related to opening ourselves courageously and expansively. The story tells of some acorns who had become so enamored with polishing and protecting their shells that they forgot that they held within the potential to become so much more than tiny acorns. It took an encounter with a muddy, cracked acorn who had lost her cap and was beginning to sprout to remind them that cracking open was key to becoming who they were meant to be—a full-grown, beautiful oak tree. In her retelling of this old story, contemplative wisdom teacher Cynthia Bourgeault reminds us that "coiled within this acorn is a vastly more majestic destiny and a true self who lives it."[2]

Breaking open and going deeper allow us to sink into our true self, a sacred reservoir of liveliness, fecundity, and interwoven connection with all beings that priest and mystic Thomas Merton referred to as a *hidden wholeness*.[3] This gift, ever-present in our souls, enables us to see more clearly and accept with compassion all of life as it unfolds. When we open to this hidden wholeness, we realize that our souls have always known who we truly are, just like the acorn who holds an oak within. As we reclaim our true essence, we embrace more fully what within us is longing to expand beyond its current confinement.

It's unclear what it costs an acorn to crack open and surrender to unfolding into their majestic destiny. However, it's likely that *our* surrender will cost us something. As we connect more deeply to our truest selves, we may sense a calling that asks more of us than we think we can give. As we slow our pace and see more clearly, we might worry that we will feel more acutely the pain and loss around us. Perhaps a change in the status quo will challenge valued relationships. We may long to keep our protective shells to avoid difficult changes we will be called on to make in our lives. It might be hard to imagine that cracking open ultimately will benefit us and the world. Still, just as the shoot pushes against the side of the acorn shell, we may hear from deep within ourselves the persistent whispers of what is bumping up against constraints, waiting to emerge.

Listening to Trees

As we slowly learn to open ourselves to the spiritual wisdom of trees, our most important practice is to pay attention. This sounds like something a teacher once told me to do as my mind wandered outside the classroom on a spring day. However, when we speak of opening to spiritual wisdom, we're talking about a deeper, more encompassing way of being in body and soul that engages our senses and tunes our mind to gentle curiosity. This is not the intense focus we often use when we attempt to solve a problem. This is a practice of deep and tender awareness: listening, seeing, sensing, and remaining present to what is, without expectation or judgment.

This contemplative practice is sometimes referred to as *a long, loving look at the real*[4]; in this space, we release any desire to judge, fix, use, or change ourselves, the situation, or others around us. In truth, we begin to realize that there are no *others*. We gaze on the world and acknowledge the unassailable connections to the Holy Mystery that weaves through and among all life and within which all life is held. Such practices focus not on explaining the sacred but experiencing it.

Through many of our experiences in school, work, and other avenues of our lives, we have learned to prize the wisdom of our minds. Yet mystics and wise ones through the ages have understood that the heart is our primary organ of perception. Today those who study the workings of the heart acknowledge that much of the information we receive from the world around us flows to the heart before being routed to the brain.

The heart as a center of spiritual perception and wisdom—*mind in heart*—is found in Christian, Jewish, and Islamic wisdom traditions. As we interact with trees, we're invited to shift from only the raw emotions of the reactive ego response, move beyond the limits of logical thinking alone, and perceive with the heart—a wordless, universal understanding of loving connection. The spiritual heart does not divide and separate to understand; the heart harmonizes by drawing on our innermost knowing.[5] We already know this heart connection through our love of others. We have experienced the wordless messages that enable us to share joy and pain at unspeakable depths.

We also sense our expanding capacity for heart knowing when we are captured by awe and wonder. Encompassed by awe, our sense of self dissolves into the experience; the ego is absorbed into a larger, transcendent web of life. Like the wise acorn, we are broken open. We feel smaller but not diminished. We know our place in the midst of things. Dacher Keltner, a professor at the University of California, Berkeley, who studies awe, wrote that it quiets the parts of our brain given to worry and rumination and enhances those parts that are more communal and compassionate. When we are awestruck by nature, our brains are no longer working in default mode. Our *self* falls silent.[6]

From this place of silent self, we are no longer a distinct bundle of personal worries but are enveloped within an all-encompassing oneness. In this space of heart and soul, we may see more clearly the hidden wholeness within every tree, within every being. The divine spark within us recognizes and honors the divine spark in others, and we find ourselves connected, soul to soul. We may be reminded of the Hindu greeting, namaste, sometimes translated as "I greet the Divine in you."

Surrounded as we are by a world of miraculous beauty, one might think it would be possible to live in a constant state of awe, wonder, and divine connection. Although beauty has the force to envelop and overcome us, it can also present itself as a gentle unfolding. As the late Irish poet and philosopher John O'Donohue noted, beauty may be "so quietly woven through our ordinary days that we hardly notice it."[7] It will require slowing our pace and drawing out our gaze so that we might notice such subtle beauty. As we do so, we may see the exquisite detail of an oak leaf or catch the tangy scent of pine. Beauty has the gentle power to draw us inward, revealing in turn the beauty within our own souls as they harmonize with the ethereal music around us.

It may be hard to imagine that we could slow our busy lives sufficiently to live in awe, wonder, and beauty. Summoning the patience to listen to trees can seem daunting in the beginning. Perhaps we've been rewarded for shell polishing for much of our life and are just beginning to respond to the invitation to break open. My longtime teacher used to say that it takes three thousand times of practice to replace an old habit with a new one. That seemed incredibly discouraging to me until I remembered that I am always practicing something. As I walk in the woods near my home and practice attentiveness, the smallest pink along the branches of the redbud is calling to me. She opens to the changing seasons with such grace and beauty—and awakens in me a longing to match my rhythm to that of the world around me.

We can continue to practice hurrying through our days with our minds on the future or stuck in the past. However, if we are to receive the spiritual wisdom of trees, if we are to be open to the holy whispers within and around us and trees, it will be important to *practice* being present, senses tuned, intentionally breathing into our heart space to call our attention there, listening for perceptions beyond words.

The redbud on my path, indeed all trees, are already engaged in this practice, living fully in each moment, serving as reminders and models of the joy and wisdom of being fully present.

Trees as Spiritual Teachers

Although scientists have recently helped to expand our understanding of trees' wise ways, the idea that trees contain deep wisdom has a long history. Ancient wisdom held that the universe was a spiral around a center; the heart of the cosmos was often depicted as the *tree of life* in which all beings were interrelated, evolving, and imbued with divine spirit.[8] Many terms that have to do with learning, knowledge, and wisdom in the Germanic languages are derived from the words for trees or woods. For example, *wit* and *wisdom* come from the ancient Scandinavian root word *vid*, which means wood or forest.

Worldwide, many religious traditions are intertwined with trees. In the ancient Celtic world, oaks were considered sacred and the origin of all knowledge. The most knowledgeable people of this community, the Druid priests, underwent twenty years of learning within and from the ancient oak forests.[9] The Buddha received enlightenment under the sacred Bodhi tree.[10] Trees are figures throughout the Christian Bible, serving as symbols, signposts, and teachers. Early Celtic Christians blended their pagan history with newly acquired theology and worshipped outdoors around stone crosses depicting scenes from the Bible on one side and the natural world on the other.

Drawing on the spiritual wisdom of trees is not exclusively an ancient practice. Current writers make a case for the importance of trees as teachers: David George Haskell, Lyanda Lynn Haupt, Belden C. Lane, and Diana Beresford-Kroeger, to name but a few. For some, it has been the practice of a lifetime.

I was drawn to eastern red cedars as a child growing up in central and western Kansas. Cedars were readily available and hardy, and that won them a place in our yard surrounded by fields of golden wheat and endless sky. I would sit in their shade, picking their small blue berries and pretending that they would be made into jam like the currants my mother picked along the roadside. I felt an attraction to this tree with its stringy red bark that was used to line the nest of squirrels and that smelled like Mother's cedar chest. The leaves were feathery and scale-like, soft to the touch as I stroked them. In winter the still-green trees were shrouded in snow, creating a glimmering wonderland and a special hideout beneath laden branches.

Although cedars appear a little ragged in comparison to other conifers, they thrive in the hot summers and brutal winters. My tree was not showy; she could hide in plain sight. But she was constant; you could count on her in any season. Her gifts were available if you knew how to look for them, and she was generous in sharing. It would be many years before I could appreciate that my cedar was sharing not only shade, berries, and a snow fort with me but also her spiritual wisdom.

When we speak of the spiritual wisdom of trees and gaining insights from them, we are speaking both metaphorically and literally. Receiving spiritual wisdom from trees in the metaphorical sense is the most straightforward and culturally accepted way to be informed by these elders. The story of the acorn presents parallels between the lives of trees and our own, and it may inspire us to deepen our own spirituality. And there are more similarities. Trees are rooted in a community; they need nourishment to grow; both light and dark are important to them; they face a wide variety of obstacles—we could go on, and we will as our conversations unfold. As we open to the possibility of learning from the spiritual wisdom of trees, we will see many examples that apply to our lives.

But trees are not only metaphors for our spiritual journey. Trees are spiritual beings—literally. My cedar could be no other than the tree she was meant to be. True to their sacred essence, trees embrace their own remarkable and unique wholeness without attempt to withhold or conceal. Author Douglas Wood wrote of a small and twisted jack pine who stood alone on a rocky point on an island that Wood loved. A silent sentinel, it spoke of "a wholeness and harmony, an integrity that comes from being what you are and belonging where you are."[11]

In the presence of such authenticity, we, too, are called to be fully ourselves. Sometimes that feels like a very tall order. Yet the immediacy of body memory—smell, taste, touch, sounds, sight—is available again to me when I still my busy mind and recall those moments lost in tree communion. Then I am able to loosen my protective shell of self-reference and sink into the sacred whole.

Later in my life, I learned that the Kiowa of the western and southern plains, as well as the Comanche, acknowledged the special spiritual significance of the cedar, regarding it as the *tree of life* or *holy tree*. It is considered one of four sacred medicines for many Nations. The berries I loved to pick take three years to turn from flower to green to the dusty blue I so admired. They provide food to more than fifty bird species. The durable wood was used in teepees, lance shafts, and other items; cedar boughs were used for bedding and bark for roofing and floor mats. The bark contributed to ceremonies and was burned in sweat lodges. In other words, many Indigenous people lived their entire lives within the full embrace of the sheltering, healing cedar—sweet medicine for body and soul.[12]

When we walk in the woods or sit with a tree and become aware of a hushed holiness, it's possible that we are sensing the sacred connections forged by people from time beyond memory and written into our very bones. It's possible that the trees have carried throughout generations their own *hidden wholeness* that speaks to us, soul to soul, beyond the bounds of words.

We may sense a sacred calling because trees are so genuinely themselves. The story I recounted of acorns choosing to maintain their shiny shells rather than plunge into the fullness of rooting in the soil is instructive, yet we know that it cannot possibly be true. Although trees face many challenges and must make choices in order to thrive, they stand firm in what they are meant to be. We are the only species who ponders and frets over who we are to become.

A Soul Friend

Our individual journey to *cracking open*, our soul journey, requires a descent to the depths of who we truly are. The late Thomas Berry, a priest and cultural historian, termed this journey *inscendence* to indicate that this is not about *transcending* beyond ourselves but rather going inward to reclaim our essence that illumines our unique role and connects us to the sacred web of life in which we live.[13] Such a journey may be a difficult one on a path lined with seductive, false doorways or a road slanted toward conformity to the dominant culture. It can be very helpful to make this journey with a wise elder who has gone before. This is the role of a teacher tree. The practice of bringing a teacher tree into your life is described in more detail in the Bringing It Home: Spiritual Practice section at the end of this chapter.

As you get to know your teacher tree intimately and deeply, she might become for you what O'Donohue describes as an *anam cara*, the Gaelic term for *soul friend*. This tradition comes from an early Celtic church practice of having someone in your life as a teacher or spiritual guide with whom you could share your innermost self—heart, mind, and soul. This was considered the deepest of friendships, one that "cut across all convention, morality, and category. One was joined in an ancient and eternal way with the 'friend of your soul.'" Feeling fully understood, it was possible to free oneself into the "trust and shelter of the other person's soul."[14] When we have the honor of serving others as their anam cara, our way of seeing is transformed; identity and perception are altered; and we become a presence in the other's life as our hearts acquire a new depth of being.

The teacher tree, my own anam cara, who found me after our latest move is a black walnut on a path near our home. Like the cedar teacher, the black walnut is constant but not showy. And there's something about how the nut-meat is encased and then encased again that I feel sure I'm meant to learn.

Since I have embraced the practice of connecting to nonhuman beings as *kin*, I try to remember not to use the term *it* to describe trees—or other living beings for that matter. My black walnut teacher tree is *monoecious*, with male and female flowers on the same tree: yellow-green male flowers, *catkins*, and white female flowers, both of which grace the tree in spring. I've chosen to refer to my teacher as *they*.

When I stretch my arms to encircle the rough and furrowed trunk of my teacher tree, I can reach only two-thirds of the way around them. They are not particularly large for a black walnut tree, possibly because similarly sized walnut trees nearby compete for the sunlight. Black walnut trees, *Juglans nigra*, usually limit competition by releasing *juglone*, a natural herbicide that reduces the growth of many shrubs. By reserving water and nutrients for themselves and given sufficient opportunity for sun, they may grow to seventy to ninety feet high with a shade-producing spread of fifty feet. Except for a darker trunk, my teacher doesn't readily distinguish themself from the ragtag band of trees and shrubs who live along the winding path through this once-neglected farmland that is now a conservation area. With no low branches remaining, the distinguishing pointed and toothed leaves are out of sight for humans passing by on the trail.

I'm still not clear how I chose this tree as my teacher. Perhaps they chose me, getting my attention by lobbing a green husked fruit my way. Certainly, those balls cover the path in autumn, and one must be careful not to turn an ankle when walking there in the dark. I've noticed how the black walnut protects their seedy essence, wrapping the nutmeat in a hard, ridged shell and then encasing the shell in a green husk destined to stain my hands should I try to remove it. It takes an eager squirrel or a cold winter to dissolve the husk so that it will easily fall away. Otherwise, it takes stomping on them, cracking them with a hammer, or giving them a long soak just to remove the husk and get to the shell. Of course, if the tree were conveniently located like the one who grew near our garage when I was very young, the husks would give way under the weight of the family car as we came and went. Then the shells could be cracked and the nutmeat picked out over long winter nights, readying them for inclusion in breads and cakes like those my mother baked.

It seems that cracking open is less straightforward for a black walnut than the acorns we discussed earlier. Walnuts remind me how easy it is to wrap my heart and soul in protective layers, holding back until the freezing and thawing of winter eventually works on me. I admire this tree who patiently persists in less-than-ideal circumstances. Although giving off leave-me-alone signals, they generously share branches with cardinals and chickadees and offer nutmeats to determined squirrels and persistent humans. I visit this tree on my wanders, pausing to look up into their branches, imagining their roots underground, wondering who they are befriending and who is being warned away. I ask them what they need. Sometimes I hear nothing. Other times I sense that simply paying attention is all that's invited.

It's important to grant ourselves patience and compassion as we engage with a teacher tree and learn new practices. Stepping outside of our comfort zones—and often outside the norms of our community—can be exciting, scary, disconcerting, and reinvigorating. Yet we are not alone; we are held within a long lineage of those who have taken this sacred journey to crack open, become deeply rooted, and connect more deeply with the living world. This lifetime pilgrimage includes no clear destination, nor even signposts, for each individual creates their path by walking. Often our paths will circle back to places we have been before, each new visit inviting us to see afresh from a richer perspective.

Although rooting into the ground of our being might be a messy process, it is in reclaiming our sacred essence that we enliven our souls and offer our unique gifts to the world. We can trust that as we become increasingly connected with our teacher tree and all other trees we encounter, we will gain strength, courage, and spiritual wisdom for the journey.

Bringing It Home: Spiritual Practice

Intention
To develop an open heart to receive the wisdom of trees and to identify a particular tree that will be your teacher for the duration of this book and beyond.

Description

Begin this practice by wandering in a wooded area close to your home—your yard, a local park perhaps, or any place that's convenient for you to visit on a regular basis. Breathe deeply. Walk slowly. See if you can synchronize your breath with your steps.

As you wander, pay attention to the trees around you. Notice the differences and similarities among them. See if there is a tree that is particularly attracting you, calling you to notice her. Ask the tree if she would be willing to be your teacher for the next several weeks or beyond. (If you prefer, ask Spirit, or other names you might have for the One, to teach you through the tree.) Over the course of reading this book, spend as much time with your tree teacher as you can. Pay attention to her and get to know her. Gaze on her from close up and from afar, listen to her, touch her, smell her. You might try to engage with her with a different sense each day.

Sit quietly with your teacher tree; perhaps lean against her trunk. Breathe with her as she absorbs carbon dioxide and gives you life-giving oxygen. Focus only on your breath and her breath. Allow thoughts to come and go—swept away with the breeze. See if you can feel the many ways that she has become open and vulnerable in her life, from the moment her seed fell to the ground. Spend some time with her in her vulnerability.

End your time with gratitude for all that she has given you and to other forest creatures and ask what you might offer to her in gratitude. Return to this tree as often as you can as you read this book.

CHAPTER 3

THE WONDER OF TREES

BETH

Trees tell a story, but only to those who know how to read it.

—Tristan Gooley, *How to Read a Tree*

Happily, I was charged with picking up my eight-year-old granddaughter from her first day of nature camp last summer. I was excited to hear the first on-the-ground report from Lucy, who had been looking forward to the camp for the entire summer. When Lucy spied me, she ran exuberantly to the car, jumped in, climbed on her booster, and clicked in her seatbelt. As was our custom, I asked Lucy what kind of music she'd like to listen to on the way home. Without hesitating, Lucy responded, "That won't be necessary, Grandma. I'll be talking."

And talk she did.

In comprehensive detail, Lucy described her day. When I finally could get a word in, I asked, "What was a favorite part?"

"Being a tree!" Lucy responded. And with continued enthusiasm, Lucy described the experience of the campers becoming the cross-section of a tree. "Well, first, some kids made a circle and then bunched together. That's the *heartwood*. That's the part that supports the tree and holds the tree up. Then some other kids made a circle around the heartwood and hopped up and down. That's the *sapwood*, where the water moves up the tree from the roots. Then some more kids made a big circle around THAT. That's where new cells are made and what makes tree rings, but I don't remember the name for it."

"Cambium," I added.

Lucy continued, slightly annoyed to be interrupted. "THEN, more kids made another skinny circle around the whatever-you-called-it, and that part of the tree is called flow-it. That's the place where the food moves from the leaves to the rest of the tree." *Phloem*, I thought, but I dared not interrupt. Her name did make some sense.

"And then all the rest of the kids formed a big circle around THAT, and they were the *bark*. And THEN the counselors tried to attack the tree. They pretended to be bugs and disease and stuff like that which can hurt the tree." Looking in the rearview mirror, I could see Lucy sitting high in her seat and leaning forward with excitement. Then she said loudly, "But the bark was really tough, and the kids fought them all off." With this, Lucy punched like a boxer. "And then the counselors all ran away because the bark had defeated them!" With this last statement, Lucy raised her arms high in victory.

As Lucy finally took a breath, I responded to the surprisingly accurate description. "Wow. It seems like you learned a lot about trees today."

Lucy replied, with more than a little disappointment in her voice, "I guess, Grandma. But mostly it was just fun!"

Why Learn About Trees?

Knowing the parts of the tree and how they grow and function can indeed be fun and fascinating. But more than just feeding our curiosity, learning about trees is an essential way to get to know them and experience them more intimately—to truly see them, better understand them, engage with them, and learn from each of them as a spiritual teacher, an anam cara that Leah described in chapter 2. We might gaze at a forest and at first see only a sea of green. But as we look more closely, we begin to pick out deciduous trees from coniferous, then oak tree from maple, then red oak from white oak. As we do, we begin to connect in an ever-deepening relationship with the trees and the sacred community to which we all belong.

In his beautiful book, *The Great Conversation: Nature and the Care of the Soul*, theologian Belden C. Lane shares a particularly close spiritual relationship he has had for decades with a tree he calls "Grandfather." Lane describes the wisdom Grandfather has provided and how important Grandfather has become to him as an expression of the holy: "My falling in love with a tree has, finally, been a profound experience of the sacred." And as he moves more deeply into this spiritual relationship, he is compelled to learn everything he can about trees—"from canopy and tree-root research to arboriculture and tree-climbing-techniques."[1]

His words strike a chord with me. Like Lane, as I fall more in love with trees and experience the sacred within them, I want to connect even more deeply by learning more about these amazing beings. In doing so, I find common ground with them. I recognize familiar patterns, processes, and challenges. After all, we process proteins the same way that trees do and produce and convert energy in a similar manner. We also come from common ancestors and have the same DNA structure.[2] As I have studied how trees live, grow, reproduce, confront challenges, collaborate, and ultimately face death, I have found not only intimate relationship with them but also an opening to holy connection with the other myriad plants, creatures, and organisms with whom I interact, as well as the enlivening force that enfolds us all.

Trees have been around for quite a bit longer than we humans have and can therefore share important experience with us. Learning how they live, grow, relate to others, and eventually die can open us to deep wisdom for our times.

Trees, like all life, had their origins in the ocean. As plant life moved from sea to land, some plants began to develop *lignin*, a hearty substance that allowed them to grow taller, reach the sun better, and develop more sophisticated vascular and root systems. Eventually, around 350 million years ago, plants with just a single woody stem evolved. We know those single-stemmed woody plants now as trees.[3]

Conifers—trees with needles (or scales) and cones—arrived on Earth first, followed by flowering, leaf-dropping deciduous trees. Trees are nature's original survivors, eventually adapting and diversifying across a variety of habitats, geographies, and elevations all around the globe. "Left to its own devices, nature comes up with trees in most situations because they win the harsh game of survival in all but the most extreme environments."[4]

While learning the ecology of trees—or any part of nature—is important, Robin Wall Kimmerer reminds us that science is only the beginning of knowledge. She tells us that we must also listen attentively to what nature itself is saying to us. In *Braiding Sweetgrass: Indigenous Wisdom, Scientific Knowledge, and the Teachings of Plants*, she tells the story of taking her class to the field when she was a newly minted professor: "I'd told them all about how it works and nothing of what it meant." Instead of allowing the land to speak for itself, she discovered that she had been "colonized by the arrogance of science" and was behaving as if she were the only one who had wisdom to share: "Paying attention is a form of reciprocity with the living world, receiving the gifts with open eyes and open heart. My job was just to lead them into presence and ready them to hear."[5]

When we study and learn the science of trees, we come to know what we don't know. Curiosity, awe, and wonder then arise. We find that external knowledge eventually fails us and internal wisdom emerges. Mystery reveals itself deep within. As we attend to trees intimately and mindfully, we recognize that they, and we, are inextricably connected within a vast sacred universe. We live within the holy.

Each Tree Has a Story

One of my favorite books, of the many available on trees and forests, is a slim publication called *Forest Forensics: A Field Guide to Reading the Forest Landscape* by ecologist Tom Wessels.[6] The author reminds us that "the story of place comes forth as the landscape reveals its experience through our careful attention. But in order to see and hear this story, we need to learn a new language—one we can use to read the landscape."[7]

Each tree has an individual, fascinating story, and a history, woven within the greater forest community. As we learn the language of her landscape, we come to know her story, and as we do, we come to know her. We might consider the history of each of our tree teachers—her origin story, her growing pains, times when she had to adapt to meet obstacles, struggles she might have had with disease and insects, other plants and animals with whom she interacts. And like our human stories, much of her story remains hidden inside her trunk or within her roots and will take some digging to uncover.

Over the last twenty years, I have been trying to unravel the story of a large black oak—*Quercus velutina*—who has touched me in ways I cannot quite articulate as she grows near our cabin in the Blue Ridge Mountains of Virginia. She is about forty feet tall, and her trunk is about two feet in diameter. Her crown is a collection of gnarled branches, which are pockmarked and peeling. I suspect that she is about a hundred years old and had her beginning as the chestnut blight was ravaging the remaining chestnut trees in the local forests.

In the entire time I have known her, she has appeared near death. Some years, no leaves appear and her branches are bare. In those times, I tell myself, "This will be the year she will finally fall." Then, the following year, I am relieved to see a collection of leaves springing forth, like the proverbial phoenix, as she is granted a temporary reprieve.

The black oak species can be distinguished from the other six hundred or so species of oaks by her thick, rough, and very dark bark, which becomes deeply furrowed as it ages. Her remaining leaves are shiny with sinuses that vary in shape and size depending on the amount of sun they receive. Her nut is easy to distinguish from that of other oaks as its cap covers most of the acorn, like a bashful child with their hat pulled down over their eyes.

Using clues provided by the tree herself, I imagine her story and am surprised by the many ways it overlaps with my own and gives me insights for my own journey. She probably began in early spring, as I did, but as a tiny embryo in a female oak flower (*pistillate*) on her mother tree that had recently received pollen blown in from a male flower (*staminate*) of another tree. This oak, like all oaks, are *monoecious*, with both male and female reproductive bodies on the same tree. In many monoecious trees, the female and male flowers cleverly stagger their arrival to avoid self-fertilization. Interestingly, androgyny and hermaphroditism are quite common in the plant and animal worlds and provide significant advantages as organisms evolve.[8]

Three months after fertilization, the oak embryo had matured into an acorn.[9] To begin her journey to becoming what she was meant to be, our acorn first had to fall from her mother tree. It was not her choice, of course, as it isn't our choice to leave the safety and comfort of our mother's womb. The slightest breeze might have unmoored her from the security of her first home. Of the millions of acorns who fall in the forest each year, she was one of the lucky ones who was not eaten by the many birds and mammals who feed on this bounty. A single mature oak produces fifty thousand acorns each year, but only a few survive.[10]

Rain and compaction embedded the acorn into the soil. Like the scruffy acorn Leah mentioned in the previous chapter, somewhere along the line, her cap fell off, making her vulnerable to the developing life within her. Under the ground, her shell began to soften, a small green shoot emerged, and she cracked open, beginning her journey to the oak she was meant to be. The middle of the acorn began pushing against the sides of her shell, which eventually was cast off, crumbled, and became part of the soil. All this time, she was nourished by internal food sources that gave her all the energy she needed until leaves could form. The little black oak's openness to her own vulnerability moves me to consider the ways in which I resist softening my own shell, shun internal sources that might provide support, and too often fail to open myself fully to what my own soulful journey might be revealing.

The acorn shoot began to push its way through the ground until she finally broke through and began her long journey toward the light, which is essential to support all her living systems. At the same time she was reaching to the light, a single root formed from what was left of her nut and began to push deeply into the soil, stabilizing the young plant. From the main root, other rootlets formed, and a complex root system expanded under her.

The small oak—not even a foot tall—then formed large, adult-sized leaves to catch as much of the light as possible since she was surrounded by taller light-gobbling elders. From her earliest beginnings, she did everything possible to reach out to the Source of her existence. Each leaf appeared on an individual stem, unlike the *compound* leaves of walnuts and hickories, which include several leaves on one stem. Even at this early stage of life, her leaves were big enough that they could provide her with all the energy she needed to grow and live, and without them, she could not have survived. Through the miraculous process of photosynthesis, the leaves captured energy from sunlight, and along with carbon dioxide from the air and water pulled from her roots, created sugars that fed and nourished her.

Even as a young oak, as soon as her leaves emerged, she began contributing to the broader community through photosynthesis, absorbing carbon dioxide from the air and producing oxygen. As a mature oak, she will absorb forty-eight pounds of carbon a year and store it safely until it is released by a damaging event, like fire, or decomposition. Each day, she will produce enough oxygen for a family of four humans![11]

While she needed light to live, our small tree didn't work twenty-four seven but rather took time to rest each sunset and through much of the fall and winter seasons. Unlike her human brothers and sisters, she intuitively understands the physical necessity of rest and renewal. For her to thrive, she knew that she needed time in the light and in the darkness and the in-between, just as we humans do.

As the oak continued to grow, her flexible green stem hardened into a sturdy wooden trunk that provided stability for her. Branches and twigs emerged, then more branches and twigs came from them as she grew wider and taller. Like all trees, the oak grew in only two ways—taller from the tips of her twigs and wider from inside her trunk.

I had an opportunity to discuss this growth habit with a precocious seven-year-old while hiking among the large beech trees in Rock Creek Park, in Washington, DC. I had been walking with young Nate for a while and sharing forest observations. Together we approached a large beech tree where several people had carved their initials into the tree's smooth bark. Over time, the initials had split open and widened but had not gotten any higher on the trees. As we paused, I asked Nate, "Why aren't those old initials way up high in the tree by now?" Nate let out a big sigh, as if to say, "Adults can be so clueless sometimes." He then said with a shrug, "Miss Beth—trees just don't work that way."

Indeed, they don't.

Inside the bark of the oak tree, all the growth within her trunk pushed out, not up. A thin layer of cells—the *cambium* layer—produced new wood each year. As the oak went dormant in late fall, the wood stopped growing and darkened. These darkened circles form those familiar growth rings that, when counted, give a pretty good idea of how old a tree is. When the black oak finally does fall and the growth rings inside her trunk are exposed, her story will reveal itself in more detail. If her rings are narrow, she didn't grow very much, indicating there was a challenge or trauma for her that year. On the other hand, if her rings are wide, circumstances were favorable and she grew heartily. Evidence of disease or intrusion might also be present in the form of cracks, streaks, or uneven growth.

In the midst of writing his many classic works, author Hermann Hesse took a moment to write a beautiful meditation on trees, in which he discusses how a tree's story might be read through her trunk:

> When a tree is cut down and reveals its naked death-wound to the sun, one can read its whole history in the luminous, inscribed disk of its trunk: in the rings of its

years, its scars, all the struggle, all the suffering, all the sickness, all the happiness and prosperity stand truly written, the narrow years and the luxurious years, the attacks withstood, the storms endured. And every young farmboy knows that the hardest and noblest wood has the narrowest rings.[12]

The tree offers an important lesson—those who have withstood the most, who have grown the most slowly under the most difficult circumstances, are the strongest and hardiest and most prepared to endure whatever circumstances they meet.

As the black oak slowly grew older, she created a large spreading canopy, a wondrous place that is often underappreciated. Margaret Lowman, or "Canopy Meg" as she is affectionately known, has dedicated her career to the study and preservation of forest canopies. She has found that nearly half of all living things on land make their home in the canopy of trees. As scientists are just discovering the influence of tree canopies on the ecological health of the forest, we are reminded that so much that is wondrous and important happens beyond our sight and beyond our knowing.[13]

As her canopy spread, the oak's roots were growing even faster through the soil and would eventually be at least two to four times as wide as her mature crown.[14] These roots provide essential stability and foundation and move water and important minerals from the ground up through the entire tree. In *The Hidden Life of Trees*, forester and author Peter Wohlleben calls the roots "the brain of the tree," as they orchestrate a complex chemical process that regulates the health of the entire tree.[15] Recent studies suggest that the extensive root system connects with complex fungal networks, allowing our oak to share nutrients, water, and warning signals with other forest organisms, such as other oaks, maples, dogwoods, hickories, huckleberries, smilax, fungi, and lichen.[16]

As the oak tree matured, she formed female and male flowers and produced thousands of her own acorns. Every few years, in autumn, she participated in *mast years*, those times when oaks drop acorns in massive numbers all at once. In these years, she overwhelms the predator population by producing more nuts than they can possibly eat, thereby ensuring that adequate supplies of acorns will survive. In off years, the clever oaks hold back their supply of acorns, which results in starving predators such as voles, moles, squirrels, and some larger birds. When the mast years then arrive, the acorns' chances of success are heightened by a smaller predator population.

As each winter approached, the black oak shed many of her leaves and without struggling, as we might, went into a dormant, restful state. But like other oaks and beech trees, she held onto some of her leaves throughout much of the winter. This *marcescence* remains one of nature's many mysteries. Scientists theorize that it might have something to do with protecting tender exposed buds from gnawing predators, such as deer, but they do not know for sure.[17] I find comfort in the fact that, as much as we know about the science of trees, there are still mysteries to be experienced and curiosities to be explored.

While we consider the oak's individual story, she of course does not stand alone. Her story, like all our stories, is woven into a complex and intricate tapestry, an ecosystem that supports her and is supported by her. Her forest ecosystem includes all the plants, animals, and other organisms living in a specific area around her, as well as the soil, water, air, and topographic features. She is one of many oaks in what forest ecologists call an *oak-hickory forest*, common in the Blue Ridge Mountains. Her forest probably established itself when another significant eastern forest type—the vast chestnut forests that once blanketed the east—was being eliminated by a pernicious blight. She now lives among, and has a relationship with, many other oaks, such as red, scarlet, white, and ironically the chestnut oak. Her other tree neighbors include bitternut and pignut hickories, dogwood, red maple, black gum, and an occasional tulip tree.

Throughout her life within her forest home, the oak has interacted with, and been habitat for, thousands of other living things. According to entomologist and ecologist Doug Tallamy, oaks are so essential for a stable bird diet that "any birder worth her salt already knows where to look for spring migrants: look to the oaks."[18] Among the wide variety of birds I have routinely observed flittering in the branches of the black oak are blue jays, titmice, chickadees, three species of woodpeckers, white-throated and song sparrows, various warblers and hawks, and an occasional bald eagle. I have watched squirrels and chipmunks scampering up and down her trunk and seen evidence on the ground near her of raccoons, foxes, voles, rabbits, deer, turkey, and black bear among the many vertebrates who might feast on her acorns. Some scratching of her soil has revealed salamanders, termites, worms, and many other tiny forest creatures.

Just as it is in our human communities, some members assist and others can harm. Some of the forest birds, animals, and bugs she hosts aid in her growth and the spread of her acorns. Squirrels, for example, bury her acorns then forget about them, essentially planting them in the ground and giving them a good start. Others can bring disease and even death. The large oval-shaped holes of pileated woodpeckers dot her trunk like measles. In some instances, these openings allow beetles and other pests to enter and destroy important living cells. Spongy moths (formerly called *gypsy moths*), which were introduced from Europe in the 1800s, have wreaked havoc on oaks nationwide and might be responsible for the expansive defoliation the black oak is currently experiencing.

While the black oak's trunk has grown straight and tall, her branches tell another story. They have twisted and turned, going up and down, as she assiduously moved around obstacles in her ongoing journey to the light. As I look at the circuitous path she has taken to expose herself to the life-giving light, she reminds me that our journeys to be one with Source and Spirit are seldom straight and often require adjustments and adaptations. As I gaze at her trunk more closely, I see evidence that, along the way, she has pruned unneeded branches that are no longer serving her and would otherwise impede her ability to get to the light. I wonder about what might need pruning—attitudes, lifestyles, attachments—in our individual and collective lives as we make our own way to the Light.

Through her many challenges, infestations, and disease, the black oak has shown remarkable resilience and guides and inspires me to do likewise. She doesn't fight, but she has accepted and adapted. She has learned to heal at the wounded places and carry on. Being with this tree as she confronts disease, infestation, storm events, and other intrusions has opened me to intimate connection with her. As I get to know this beautiful, broken individual, and stand with her through all her challenges, my compassion grows not only for her but also for my other nonhuman and human neighbors. And for myself. As I learn with and from her, her authentic journey invites me to live more fully into the Holy Mystery.

The Story Doesn't End

The black oak tree near our Blue Ridge cabin has been declining since I first met her. Each year, branches produce fewer and fewer leaves. Again I think, "This will be her time." She knows that she is at the mercy of her environment and she accepts this. I am having a harder time. For now, we both wait.

Perhaps next year, or ten or twenty years from now, my oak friend will stop living, as we all must someday. Before she falls to the ground, recent studies suggest that she will release much of her remaining mineral and nutrient contents to the surrounding forest, in particular to her own kin, fortifying the next generation.[19] After she falls, and if she is left undisturbed by human hands, she will remain on the forest floor and serve as a *nurse log*, continuing to nurture the forest plants and animals in new ways. Soon, moss and fungus will cover her decaying trunk. Termites and roly-polys will eat away her bark and soften her wood, opening it up to be used by larger creatures, such as salamanders and rodents. Woodpeckers will peck at her trunk in search of insects. Bears will tear off sections of her bark as they look for a meal of grubs and bugs.

Eventually, an acorn or seed of another tree will fall onto her softened wood and sprout into a new sapling. Years will go on, and she will continue to decay. At some point, she will no longer be visible, having completely degraded into soil, which will in turn serve as a place for future acorns to grow. By then, the sapling who grew from her trunk might be a healthy tree that appears to be bow-legged, her roots wrapped around an invisible *ghost tree.*

Even though our oak will no longer be visible, her essence will continue on. Her molecules will be scattered and intermingled with other elements within the forest ecosystem as she continues to nurture and serve as part of the Holy Mystery.

Bringing It Home: Spiritual Practice

Intention
To deepen attention to, and connection with, trees through spiritual nature journaling.

Description
Spiritual nature journaling can be an enjoyable and important way to build more intimacy with your teacher tree, and all trees, by noticing and recording your obser-vations. Don't worry if you've had no luck with journal-ing in the past. Spiritual nature journaling can offer a new perspective on both nature and journaling.

Before you visit your teacher tree, you might choose or make a journal that speaks to you. Prepare a cover page the depicts your intention for the time in which you are journeying with your teacher tree. Each time you visit her, consider bringing your journal with you.

Take a few centering breaths when you first reach your teacher tree and settle in before journaling. You might begin your journal by entering the date and time, then record the physical weather—temperature, precipitation, cloud cover, humidity—as well as your emotional weather—your mood and your current concerns, worries, joys, and distractions. Then slowly survey your teacher from top to bottom, side to side. Notice shapes, patterns, and colors, as well as elements that interest you or raise questions. Note how many shades of green or brown are present. Make some notes of these observations. Be curious—ask yourself why something is the way it is.

Observe other creatures or plants who are on or around your teacher. You might establish a key, with specific symbols for birds, insects, plants, etc. Regardless of your skills, you might try your hand at drawing; doing so can enhance your observation. Remember: the object of this exercise is to engage with the tree, not to hang your drawing in the Louvre. Even a stick figure (maybe *particularly* a *stick* figure) can enhance observation.

Notice also what might be stirring within you—emotions, insights, intuitions. Make note of those too. Try drawing those insights. Choose colors or shapes to describe what you are experiencing. Sometimes you only have time to make some rough sketches in the field. You can come back to your journal and fill it in later.

Spiritual nature journaling is a wonderful practice for engaging the trees with both head and heart.

CHAPTER 4

SOIL
THE GROUND OF OUR BEING

BETH

How can I stand on the ground every day and not feel its power? How can I live my life stepping on this stuff and not wonder at it?
—WILLIAM BRYANT LOGAN, *DIRT*

When I was studying forestry some years ago, I happily attended each of my classes, eager to learn more about the trees I had come to love. Well, I happily attended *most* of my classes. At eight o'clock on Monday mornings, with the help of two different alarms and a dedicated roommate, I dragged myself out of bed to attend the required course on soil science. What on earth did soils have to do with anything that I loved about trees? Is this necessary? (You might be asking yourself the same questions right now.)

The course was taught by a soil scientist who was quite well known for the brilliance of his research but not so much for the excitement of his teaching. He spoke in a mumbly monotone and sometimes seemed less interested than I was to be there. The weeks crawled by with long lists of surface and subsurface horizons—*duripan, fragipan, placic,* and *sombric*—along with discussions of complicated chemical processes that taxed my vague memory of high school science. Many in the class were enraptured. I was not. And I must admit that my attendance in the class was far from perfect.

Many years later, when my young friend Mason was completing his forestry studies at the same university, I asked about his favorite subjects. Forest ecology, dendrology, entomology? To my amazement, he quickly replied, "Soils!" After I failed to share his enthusiasm for the subject, he thought he might convince me of its allure by mailing me his 1,046-page textbook—*The Nature and Properties of Soils*—along with a note urging me to read it.[1] Ugh.

Obligatorily, I flipped through some of the pages to see if the science of soils had changed much in the intervening decades. Some of the old concepts triggered that same sense of eye-glazing they had many years ago. Before I put it down, however, I noticed a section entitled "Functions of Soils in our Ecosystem." I was intrigued. I read on. And on.

Having now read many works on forest soils, I find myself unimaginably fascinated by the role that this mysterious underground world plays in the health of forests and all natural ecosystems, as well as its importance to our spiritual lives. This statement in a well-respected forest ecology text particularly intrigued me: "The importance of soil to forest productivity and health cannot be overstated . . . [S]oil is the fundamental resource of terrestrial ecosystems that ultimately provides the substance for all earthly organisms."[2] The *fundamental* resource, providing the *substance* for *all* life. As a naturalist and great lover of trees, how could I have possibly not appreciated the importance of the foundation for all life in the forest? I would like to blame the early Monday class, but I can't.

I wasn't paying attention. I was mesmerized by the wonder and beauty of the forest and very curious about the intriguing above-ground processes, but I was unwilling to go beneath the surface, beyond my sight, and outside of my experience.

I have since learned that half of the mass of a tree is underground. What happens in the dark, often damp, mysterious underground is crucial to the functioning of the tree and the forest as a whole. Yet how often on a forest walk do we take a deep breath, look around, and say, "Wow. Dirt!" Often what is unseen lies unexperienced. We naturally assume what we can see and touch and hear is the limit to our world when there is so much mystery to be explored beneath.

What Is Soil and How Did It Emerge?

When I was first learning—or relearning—about forest soil, I was surprised to discover how much of healthy soil is open space. While soil appears to be solid, half of it is actually made up of millions of tiny spaces where water and gases are stored and transported. These *pores* are quite small, with a whopper *macropore* coming in at 0.003 inches, or about the size of the point of a pin. While they are not visible to the unaided human eye, these microscopic spaces are the heart and soul of soil, allowing it to breathe and transfer materials.[3]

We might think of soil as a very holey sponge. As long as it is damp and supple, solutions can move through it easily. If it becomes hard and dry, it can no longer do the job of absorbing and transporting essential materials.

The other half of healthy soil is mostly minerals essential to tree growth. Organic material—living or formerly living material—makes up only 5 percent of soil but is a very important part of the package. This organic material provides the tree with essential nutrients it needs to live and thrive. Rich, decomposed forest detritus, or *topsoil*, is concentrated in the upper levels of the soil. Also known as *humus*, it comes from the same root as both *human* and, interestingly, *humble*. This etymology reflects our long-standing human relationship with, and dependence on, soil.

While most of us don't think much about soil while we are digging into a sumptuous meal—pun intended— virtually all our food comes directly from the ground or from animals who have consumed food from the ground. Unfortunately, because of intensive agriculture, commercial forestry, mining, development, and the impacts of climate change, our soil is in serious trouble. A full one-third of the world's arable soil is considered degraded. This fact is particularly alarming considering the soil's slow pace of renewal. It takes about one thousand years to build about a half inch of soil.[4]

I used to think that soil had been around pretty much forever, but I discovered that Earth spent close to 90 percent of its existence without soil. And trees played an important role in soil's beginnings. Earth was originally formed about 4.5 billion years ago. Up until about 500 million years ago, the dry part of Earth was just rocky, dusty, and desolate. There was no soil on Earth, and life was confined to the waters.

At some point, mysteriously, algae began to creep out of the water and onto land and, with the help of fungi, found its footing. With time, it began to cover Earth's surface and evolved into more complex plant life. Early trees emerged. As trees and other plants died, their detritus was deposited in the crags and cracks of the rocks, in turn supporting the development of more complex plants. This decaying plant material combined with the eroding rock, and soil was born. As deciduous trees evolved, millions of decayed fallen leaves further nurtured the soil. Trees and soils are intertwined in "a dance of mutual creation."[5] More trees, more decay, more soil.

As soil developed, everything changed on Earth—not just on the surface but in the air and waters as well. Organisms crept out of the waters and found a nurturing environment on land. Early on, soil was home to a wide array of fungi, nematodes, and mites. Soil makes all earthly life possible—from large mammals to the smallest bacterium to every tree that ever existed.

About one hundred million years after the first soils developed—a short interval in geologic time—forests took advantage and spread widely over the Earth's surface. The properties of a given soil determine the kinds of trees that can grow at a particular place and determine their ultimate health and longevity.

The Functions of Soil

Nurture
First and foremost, soil provides the pathways through which trees absorb and transfer essential substances within and around the tree, as well as to other trees in

the forest. The tiny pore spaces scattered throughout the soil provide a complex system of tiny tunnels, bridges, and trails through which the tree receives the nutrition she needs. Traffic moves two ways on this highway system. The roots absorb water, needed by the tree to retain structure and run the engine of photosynthesis, from the ground. They also absorb important minerals and send those back up the trunk to be used by the entire tree. Simultaneously, sugars from photosynthesis provided by the leaves to the rest of the tree travel down the trunk to nurture the root system.

At the end of tree roots are millions of microscopic hairs. Through chemical processes, these tiny hairs seek out and absorb mineral nutrients. Helping in absorption of materials are the fungal networks, which will be discussed in more detail in chapter 7. Tree root hairs intersect with the hyphae of the fungi to form complicated mycelial networks that allow the transfer of nutrients, water, and even warning signals between trees and between trees and other plants. The complex interaction between tree roots and fungi is only beginning to be understood but already expands our understanding and appreciation of the role that soils play in healthy forest ecosystems.

Science affirms the importance of soil to us humans as well. After all, through the intake of food, our bodies are made up of nutrients and water that primarily come from the ground. Microscopic pieces of the creatures (e.g., bugs and worms) that have crawled through the soil, as well as the many leaves that have nurtured it, are inside of us! Not surprisingly then, we have an old and visceral relationship with the soil. It connects us to a time and place in which we quite literally lived more grounded in earth. Ecopsychologists argue that this ancient connection with earth travels within our DNA and through our *ecounconscious*. Is it any wonder that recent studies from the National Institutes of Health have shown that the smell of soil is calming and restorative?[6]

For thousands of years, spiritual writers have recognized the significant physical relationship humans have with soil, which in turn informed our spiritual relationship with soil. Our ancestors in faith wrote during times when food was scarce, and it took enormous effort to grow or find food. They understood more clearly than we do now that our very existence relies on the ground.

In the oldest of the two creation stories in Genesis, the Scripture writers wrote that God actually created the human directly from the soil. In the story, God picked up some dirt—the Hebrew *Adamah*—and blew into it and created the human Adam from the dirt. In Jewish and Christian theology, our first human name was *person of the earth*. We are, according to the Bible, literally people of the dirt, brought to life by God's very breath (Gen 2:7).

James Weldon Johnson, prominent early twentieth-century Black poet, playwright, activist, and hymn-writer, interpreted the Scripture in his beautiful and popular poem "The Creation." In the poem, he described God as kneeling "down in the dust" and working it like clay. He ends the story with this poignant stanza:

Then into it he blew the breath of life,
And man became a living soul.[7]

The *breath of life* was blown into the dirt to create the human and eventually all the other creatures who roam the earth. But not just breath. The Hebrew word used in this passage is *ruach*, the same word for breath, wind, and Spirit. The Scripture writers made no distinction. According to Johnson and the Scripture writers, we are a cosmic stew of soil, breath, wind, and Spirit.

Well-known twentieth-century theologian Paul Tillich, whose life was steeped in nature, routinely referred to God as the "ground of being," in which all creatures—human and nonhuman—have their being.[8] Having now come to appreciate soil more, the *ground* of being seems a particularly helpful guide to our spiritual seeking. As we search for Divine Mystery, we, like the tiny root hairs searching for nutrients, are looking for something that is not necessarily on the surface of our experience but grounded, rooted, outside our normal sightlines. And remaining open-hearted and spacious and avoiding compaction are essential to the search for both soil nutrients and Spirit.

Soil Breathes

Science now affirms the sense of the Scripture writers that breath and soil are interconnected. As I delved further into soil, I was surprised to learn that soil respirates in much the same way we do. Oxygen travels from the air into the ground through the network of pores and is therefore made available for use by soil organisms. Oxygen circulating through the many dark layers of soil provides life to the millions of creatures who live there, allowing them to eat, mate, provide countless services to the earth and other creatures, and finally die.

Just as soil organisms take in oxygen, they release carbon dioxide as a waste product through the same pathways. And when they die and decay, more carbon dioxide is produced. Soil is therefore an extremely important storehouse for this greenhouse gas. In fact, more carbon is stored in soil than in all the plants and the air combined.[9]

Clearing forests for agriculture, grazing, timber, development, mining, and other purposes disturbs the forest soils and releases tons of carbon dioxide that further exacerbates the enormous challenge of climate change. Studies indicate that clearing trees for agriculture alone has resulted in the release of fifty to one hundred gigatons of carbon into the air since the time of the Industrial Revolution.[10] The maintenance of healthy forest soils will therefore play a significant role in mitigating the impacts of a dangerously warming Earth.

Connections

Not only does soil have a significant role in providing nurture—physical and spiritual—but it is also essential to the movement and absorption of water. Soil scientists maintain that "nearly every drop of water in our rivers, lakes, estuaries, and aquifers has either traveled through the soil or flowed over its surface."[11]

The extensive root system of trees acts as a giant sponge and provides essential filtering of harmful pollutants as well as absorbing and slowing floodwaters. Consequently, the removal of trees has been identified with increased flooding and erosion, and stormwater management efforts almost always include the protection and restoration of local forests.

Tree roots also regulate water flow throughout the forest and provide a spongy holding tank of water that allows the trees to have water when they need it. Before deciduous forests leaf out in the spring, the soil absorbs and holds spring rains for use later in the season. As leaves appear and then grow rapidly, sufficient water is therefore available to fuel the important process of photosynthesis. As tree roots continue to absorb water to keep the tree in good supply, healthy soil will retain enough moisture to be used in times of drought.

Soil also supports a dazzling diversity of forest organisms. Scientists estimate that a handful of soil contains billions of organisms, of all shapes and sizes and functions, that contribute not just to the health of the forest ecosystem but also to life as we know it. Groundhogs, moles, earthworms, termites, ants, beetles, millipedes, and countless microorganisms and bacteria all play important roles. Larger creatures digging in the soil provide much-needed space in the soil that would otherwise be compacted. Similarly, ants, termites, and small worms provide pathways that aerate the soil and assist in decomposing the vast amount of organic material coming from leaves, dead plants, and animals. Imagine the tons of material that would be piled up on the forest floor if these decomposers were not at work.

Smaller microscopic organisms and bacteria further break down minerals and organic matter to small-enough form to be absorbed by the tree roots and integrated into tree tissue for its future use. Bacteria also break down nitrogen into a form that can be used by the tree.

The soil organisms work in mutuality and reciprocity with the tree. The tree is dependent on the organisms to break down nutrients to a usable form, and the forest soil in turn provides the nutrients and home that the organisms require. The forest ecosystem is absolutely dependent on these connections, which will be discussed more fully in chapter 7. For now, let's recall Paul Tillich's view that God was not a being per se but the ground of *all being*, which included everything living and nonliving within the soil, on the earth, in the waters, in the air, and beyond.

I am embarrassed to admit that, for too many autumns, I didn't recognize these connections and spent many hours raking up the huge volume of leaves that fell from the oak trees in our yard. (And if I wasn't around, my husband would simplify the job by taking out the forbidden leaf blower from its hiding place in the garage.) We dutifully bagged the leaves, to be taken away by the county to points unknown. I can only imagine the millions of tiny insect and butterfly eggs and countless other organisms we killed or relocated due to our efforts to beautify our landscape. We now know better and just let the leaves pile up in the yard so they can still offer a home to the extraordinary numbers of organisms and continue to nurture the soil.

Stability

While scientists are just beginning to unearth (pun intended) some of the ecological mysteries that lie beneath Earth's surface, they do know that soil plays an essential role in providing structure for the trees by providing a home to complex, stabilizing root systems. As we've mentioned before, the roots of trees are often as wide as the tree is tall. Imagine the weight of a backyard oak that must be supported, let alone that of an enormous redwood tree. Tree roots are a tangled mess of large, medium, and small appendages that cling to the soil to support the tree. Roots of one tree combine with that of others to increase stability. A look at a recently blown-down tree reveals the Gordian knot that tried to keep the tree from toppling.

Some years ago, we bought a home in a suburban neighborhood of Washington, DC, in large measure because we fell in love with the enormous oaks that lined the street. We were captivated by one huge oak tree that loomed over the street, convincing us that this was the house for us. At sixty feet high and four feet in diameter, she towered over the neighborhood. Everyone loved this majestic being.

As she continued to grow, her roots spread under the street and our sidewalk and driveway. Our concrete surfaces were no match for the large roots, which caused some challenging undulations. We loved the majestic tree, but we didn't like the look of the wavy driveway and sidewalk in our otherwise then-manicured landscape.

Not wanting to disturb the oak but wanting to preserve our driveway and sidewalk, we consulted a number of "experts" and determined that we would move the driveway and sidewalk to curve around the tree and her major roots. It was quite an expensive and challenging undertaking, requiring heavy ground-moving machinery. We wanted to save the tree but meet our human aesthetic desires as well.

A few months later, we were out of town when we received an urgent message from our neighbor that "our" beloved oak had fallen. Other than taking out four cars along the street, there was little loss of property and no injuries. Still, we were heartbroken. And frankly, a little annoyed. We had gone to such effort to work with the tree and "save" her, only to be rewarded by her crashing down and causing an enormous mess.

After the tree fell, my husband and I engaged in a spirited series of conversations about why she died and what we could do to "fix" the other oaks in the yard so they wouldn't meet a similar fate. Yes, there had been large storms in the area. Yes, there might have been disease. Yes, trees, like all of us, have limited lifespans. But the Bobcat machine that our contractor used to move large amounts of soil around probably disturbed the soil structure and cut roots so significantly that the tree couldn't survive.

In the intervening twenty-five years since the oak fell, several additions have gone up in the neighborhood, causing increased soil erosion. Sewer work has disturbed root structures. More aggressive storms frequently flood our yards. Local arborists have convinced folks to let them take down trees that might be safety hazards, removing the structural help from neighbor trees. Now almost every one of those big beautiful oaks we admired so much is gone. And, at our house, our driveway and sidewalk still curve to wind around a tree that is no longer there—a constant reminder of the limits of our human wisdom.

Every winter solstice, I go for a walk in the forest. I begin in the late afternoon and travel through dusk into chilly darkness, stopping along the way to consider what spiritual insights various stages of light might offer. When I am finally surrounded by total darkness in the depths of the winter woods, oddly enough, I always think about fireflies, those sparkly summer creatures. I remember how Gayle Boss, in her beautiful book about Advent, explains the life cycle of a firefly. When the summer light begins to fade, fireflies lay their eggs on the ground and shortly thereafter die. Through late summer and into fall, the firefly eggs that are not eaten by hungry predators are slowly embedded in the ground. By winter, they are safely nestled in the soil. Yet even in this larval state, during which they hide in the little spaces within the dark earth, the tiny fireflies are still lightly flickering.[12]

Steeped in darkness, I wriggle my hiking books in the dirt in hopes of conjuring up the light show below. I see it so clearly in my mind. The ground below me comes alive with microscopic bursts of light. Year after year, I can almost feel the young fireflies tickling my feet. I stand in the dark woods for a while, enjoying the presence below my feet. After a while, a sense of extraordinary calm envelops me in the darkness. The presence of light where we assume there is none, invisible but imaginable, comforts and reassures me.

So much of essential forest functioning happens right under our feet, in the darkness, beyond our seeing. It provides stability, nurture, movement, breath. As soil is making these many contributions in the present, perhaps its greatest gift is to our collective futures. This *ground of our being* is also *the ground of our becoming*. At this very moment, as mammals, birds, worms, insects, microorganisms, trees, and plants are dying and decaying, soil is slowly being made and remade, providing life for millions of humans and nonhumans for thousands of years to come.

Bringing It Home: Spiritual Practice

Intention
To encounter soil as a pathway to deepening experience with our teacher tree and those whom she encounters in the soil.

Description
Walk slowly to your teacher tree. See if you can match your breath with your steps. As you do, pay attention to your

feet and feel the ground beneath you. If you are comfortable with doing so, take off your shoes and walk barefoot, taking in the soil under your feet. Pause occasionally, close your eyes, and imagine all the life in the ground below you. Imagine the complex underground pathways moving the nutrients and water that the trees and other beings need. Picture the tiny worms, insects, and microscopic organisms crawling around. Remember that our bodies include the remnants of everything and everyone who has been in soil.

When you arrive at your teacher tree, sit down with her. Notice the branches and twigs, dead leaves, and other detritus you see around you that will one day become soil. Take in the amount of decay that had to occur so that your teacher tree might have life. Dig around in the dirt and pick up a handful of soil. Close your eyes and smell deeply.

If you are inclined, write a haiku about your experience with the soil. This ancient form includes a first line of five syllables, a second line of seven syllables, and a third line of five syllables. See what comes up for you. These short poems can reveal important truths.

Chapter 5

WATER
SCREAMING TREES AND TREE-CLIMBING FISH

BETH

On the surface water can be seen as food, a means of transport, a ground for recreation or an element for cleansing, purification, and initiation in cultural ceremonies. But a deeper analysis into the values of water reveals that water is a sacred being that holds life on earth.

—Chief Tamale Bowya,
"Listening to the Spirit of Water"

As I write this chapter, it is raining. Again. Looking out my window, I notice the elm branch that frames my view. Tiny drops of water cling tightly to his twigs, next to fuzzy little green flowers that are just beginning to bloom. As my view widens, I watch the rain as it seems to bounce off the serviceberry, her limbs white and puffy with new foliage. The large red maple across the street is shiny with his watery coat.

I watch as rainwater hits the ground, then suddenly disappears, a process of absorption that I had, until just this moment, taken for granted. I imagine the water then being taken in by the roots of the elm, serviceberry, and maple to give structure and stability to the trees and to provide the substance by which all nutrition is produced and through which all nutrition is transported. As I see water touch every natural thing in my sight, I remember that water does indeed touch everything.

There's Something about Water

Some years ago, I participated in a program on the spirituality of water at a suburban church in an affluent town outside of Washington, DC. The church's property extended down a short, steep hill, at the bottom of which was a small creek that fed into the main source of drinking water for the town. At the beginning of the program, a group of about twenty congregants and the pastor gathered at the top of the hill. I watched as my friend Santo, a prominent businessman in the community, shuffled his feet. I guessed he had been, let's call it, *encouraged* to come to the event by his wife.

We walked slowly down the hill until we reached the glistening stream, which was surrounded by silver maples and sycamores. As we arrived there, one participant said, "Oh, my! I haven't been down here since the kids were little. It's so beautiful." Others shared similar sentiments. For most, "church" had always been inside the building, despite water being so significant to Christian tradition.

We then got to know the stream through the spiritual practice of using our senses. Each of us used a specific sense—hearing, smell, sight, or sound—with which we experienced the stream. I watched with surprise as the group fully engaged with the exercise, wading into the stream with joyful shrieks and giggles.

After the practice was over, most of the group shared their experiences. Some commented on how the stream had touched them, others on how they were reminded of their baptisms. Some expressed regret that they had ignored this lovely creek for so long. The pastor expressed her view that the church's *sanctuary* should extend to the natural area around the church, including this beautiful stream and woodland. Finally, there was a pause, and it seemed that all who wanted to share had done so.

I looked over to Santo, whose eyes were glistening with tears. His voice cracking, he slowly spoke: "When I closed my eyes and listened to the creek, I was transported right back to a little stream in Carisolo, the Italian village where I was born and have returned to many times. I could see everything—the hills, the Alpine firs, and . . ." Here he paused and then continued haltingly: "And I could see my late father, who loved fishing that stream and regaling me with stories from his youth. I loved thinking of him there."

There is something about water.

It connects, deepens, lifts, anoints, purifies. It dissolves stone and earth, as well as the boundaries of time and geography. It seeps into the hardest ground and into the most guarded heart.

We know this. When we sit by a forest stream, watch the ocean waves roll in, or paddle a mountain lake, we are quieter, calmer, at peace, at home. Perhaps we know viscerally how precious water is, that 60 percent of our bodies are made of it, and that we cannot go more than a few days without it. Perhaps we carry the memory of a time when life-giving water was scarce, even though many of us (but certainly not all) can now access water with a pull on the tap. Perhaps the waters of our mother's womb, our first home, still ripple within us.

Sacred Waters

Given our visceral connections to water, it is not surprising that it has been fundamental to our spiritual searching for thousands of years. Often living in lands that were arid and drought ridden, our spiritual ancestors marveled at the precious waters coming from the sky and from under the ground. They wondered who or what had provided them the life-giving water. What spirit, gods, or God was the source of this gift? Rooted in its physical necessity, water has become part of our spiritual DNA. This source of life became our Source of life.

Every major spiritual tradition understands water as sacred. In Hinduism, the Ganges River has great significance, as it both purifies and holds the essence of Hindu wisdom. For Buddhists, water is considered one of the five life-giving elements, and the Buddha encouraged exercising restraint in its use as well as sharing generously. The Qur'an states clearly that water is a life-giving gift of Allah and everything is made from it. As such, it is to be protected, used with restraint, and not defiled. For Jews and Christians, water plays a significant role throughout their Scriptures. In the Biblical creation story, Earth itself emerged right from the waters. In countless other passages, God appears in watery forms—fountain, stream, sea, storm.

While traditions vary among different groups, Indigenous peoples have long understood water to be sacred.

Many Indigenous creation stories involve water and floods. Water also serves a role in purification and cleansing rituals and is a significant part of other ceremonies.[1] Particular water bodies are considered sacred to specific nations and worthy of protection. From 2016 to 2017, the Lakota and Dakota nations fought to protect the Missouri River, the source of their drinking water, from the damaging impacts of the Dakota Access Pipeline, which would carry crude oil underneath the river. Despite large-scale demonstrations drawing thousands of people and widespread media cover, the pipeline was eventually built and is operational today.

We are challenged to fully appreciate the spirituality of water when we realize that access to clean water is far from equitable. In fact, two billion people, over 25 percent of the world's population, lack access to safe drinking water.[2] Even here in the United States, clean water is not a guarantee, particularly for marginalized communities. In 2014, city officials in Flint, Michigan—primarily a community of color with a high poverty rate—decided to save money by switching water supplies. Soon after, high concentrations of lead and other dangerous substances were found in the water, causing serious illness and harm, particularly to children. Years have passed, and the safety of Flint's water is still in question.

Life-Giving Water and Screaming Trees

Water as the Source of life is not limited to humans. It is essential to every organism on Earth, including trees. In fact, half of the volume of a tree is water. Purdue University instructor Lindsey Purcell wrote: "Water is the single most limiting ecological factor in tree growth and survival. Without adequate water, a tree's functions will quickly decline, and then die."[3]

Along with energy from the sun and carbon dioxide from the air, water is an essential ingredient in photosynthesis, which provides the fuel for all the tree's cell growth. Without enough water, photosynthesis in the leaves and needles simply shuts down. Water is also necessary to transport the nutrients created by photosynthesis to the rest of the tree through the *phloem* (or "flow-it," as young Lucy called it).

With water, trees participate in the underground fungal networks that allow them to share nutrients and minerals with other trees and plants. Studies have found that trees sometimes provide water needed by fungi in exchange for needed nutrients. This process is particularly important during dry weather, when nutrients cannot move around as freely.[4] Water also keeps the tree trunk, bark, branches, twigs, and internal structure supple. If a tree's bark and wood crack, the tree opens to invasions from destructive fungi and insects.

A tree will do anything to get water and keep it. When I visited the Desert Botanical Museum in Phoenix, I was fascinated to learn the extent to which a tree will go to access and retain water under the most challenging circumstances. Just as animals stockpile food, trees stockpile water in their trunks and roots. Desert trees can go long stretches without water and tend to have smaller, waxy leaves that prevent evaporation. They also have broader root systems to absorb water when it comes and long taproots for plumbing the depths for underground reservoirs. And some trees, like the paloverde, simply turn themselves off in drought conditions, drop their leaves, and wait for rain. I thought at first that this process might limit photosynthesis until I noticed the tree's green bark. The paloverde cleverly photosynthesizes through her trunk as needed.

Water is so precious to trees that if they don't have enough of it, they actually scream! If the flow of water from the roots to the leaves is interrupted, the trunk will start to vibrate and make low-level noise that can be picked up ultrasonically. What's the purpose of this screaming? Are the trees sending distress signals to other trees in the forest? For now, arboreal screaming will remain part of the mystery that surrounds much of what we don't know about trees.[5]

Does Water Flow Uphill?

When we pause for a moment to consider how the precious water moves through the various parts of a tree to nourish her, we are both confounded and amazed. Like so much that is mysterious and mystical, most of the hydrology of a tree is in the interior, in the dark, and hidden from our view.

The engine that drives water movement through a tree is the leaf. Through transpiration, leaves draw water and minerals from the roots through tiny capillaries within the *xylem* of the trunk. These miniature straws can be as small as 0.02 inches in deciduous trees and in conifers, a minuscule 0.0008 inches.[6] The leaf draws water from the roots up through the trunk to fuel photosynthesis, which in turn releases oxygen into the air. A one-hundred-foot tree with about two hundred thousand leaves can pull eleven thousand gallons of water from the soil in one growing season.[7] David George Haskell, the author of several books on the wonder of trees, remarks: "If humans were to design mechanical devices to lift hundreds of gallons of water from roots to canopy, the forest would be a cacophony of pumps . . . Evolution's economy is too tight and thrifty to allow such profligacy, so water moves through trees with silence and ease."[8]

Most scientists believe that surface tension within the small capillaries of the xylem provides enough internal pressure for transpiration seemingly to defy gravity by pumping large volumes of water up the tree. Yet others are skeptical about whether the surface tension of the tiny capillaries can possibly explain how water is lifted a hundred or more feet in the air. In the minds of these scientists, transpiration remains a mystery.[9]

Is gravity-defying transpiration just a process that is yet unexplained by science, or is there something else at play? Regardless of whether transpiration is a scientific puzzle just waiting to be solved definitively or part of a larger mystery that moves through natural life-giving processes, an exploration of it invites us into a deeper relationship with both the tree and the water that gives her life. As the title of Iris DeMent's poignant song says, I think I'll "Let the Mystery Be."

We have a family mystery in the water of our woodland pond near the black oak I mentioned in chapter 3. When my grandchildren visited last spring, they spent many happy hours by and in the pond, which was nearly overflowing its banks. They gleefully captured hundreds of tadpoles in glass jars, then watched them in wide-eyed amazement before returning them safely to the pond waters. Yet when we returned in late summer, the tadpoles and the pond water were both completely gone. Some of the water had evaporated, but most of it had been absorbed by the roots of the surrounding large oaks and maples and used to nurture the trees during their busy summer cycles.

Five-year-old Daphne was bereft. "Where did all the water go? And what happened to the tadpoles?" I reassured her that the tadpoles had turned into frogs, were living happily in the woods nearby, and would produce more tadpoles when the rains brought the pond more water in the spring. Then I engaged in a little Socratic grandmothering. "Daphne," I asked, "Where do you think all the pondwater went?" She thought for a moment, and my pragmatic suburban granddaughter responded, "I think it just went down the sewer."

Can Fish Climb Trees?

Some years ago, Albert Einstein allegedly proclaimed: "If you judge a fish by its ability to climb a tree, it will live its whole life believing that it's stupid." While this humorous musing might offer some sage advice, it also turns out that the presumption within it—that fish cannot climb trees— might not be accurate.[10]

Last summer, I witnessed one of the most remarkable spectacles I have ever observed in the natural world— brown bears fishing for salmon at Brooks Falls in Katmai National Park. I had been planning for this moment for years. I had poured over hundreds of photos, studied maps, made complicated travel reservations, and hoped the weather would cooperate. Finally, after several long flights in large and small airplanes, I was there.

When I got to the viewing platform, I couldn't take it all in. In the clear, wide Brooks River were hundreds of bright red sockeye salmon, clustered at the base of the six-foot-high Brooks Falls, where they had stopped to rest in their arduous journey upstream to reach their traditional spawning grounds. Dozens of massive bears were spread out on top of and below the falls, greedily snatching fish after fish out of the stream as the salmon tried to leap up the falls. Brown bears need to eat dozens of fish a day to fatten themselves up in preparation for the cold and dark seasons to come.

Each bear had their own style. The younger bears were aggressively stalking and grabbing any fish they could lay their claws on. An elderly bear, named Otis by the rangers, simply sat at the top of the falls, Winnie the Pooh–style, and practically waited until the salmon fell in his lap. Mama bears were feeding their young and then chasing them up the white spruce along the riverbank when hostile bears lumbered too close. And all the bears ceded ground when Grazer—a very large, aggressive female, so named because of her fishing style—arrived on the scene.

I was mesmerized. I felt a Presence, within each fish, each bear, the river, and the white spruce. Right before my eyes, I was witness to a wondrous piece of the cycle of life, all born in water. I was captivated by the interconnections between the fish, the bears, the trees, and the river, each playing an important role. What I hadn't realized at the time, however, was that the interconnections ran much deeper than I had imagined.

I have since learned that decomposing salmon along the banks of the Brooks River provide essential nutrients to the white spruce, providing as much as 70 percent of the nutrients needed by the tree. Each salmon carcass carries 4.5 ounces of nitrogen and 0.7 ounces of phosphorous, providing natural fertilizer to the ground. These salmon carcasses decay and are absorbed into the soil. Their nutrients find their way into the watery underground pathways in the roots. Amazingly, traces of salmon protein have been found in the trees! These salmon-rich trees are greatly advantaged. In the Tongass National Forest in southeastern Alaska, western hemlock and Sitka spruce grow three times faster on salmon streams than they would under other circumstances.[11]

And these fishy trees give back by providing important shade to salmon and many other species of water creatures. Dead trees left in streams and creeks provide important nooks and crannies in which fish, frogs, salamander, and insects lay eggs and hide from predators.

So it seems, Dr. Einstein, with a lift—literally—from water, fish do indeed climb trees.

Do Trees Make the Weather?

In his biography of Christopher Columbus, Columbus's son noted his father's observation that in Jamaica, an hour-long rain shower would soak the land every afternoon. The younger Columbus added that his father "knew from experience that formerly this also occurred in the Canary, Medeira, and Azore Islands, but since the removal of forests that once covered those islands, they do not have so much mist and rain as before."[12] While Columbus was wrong about so many things, on this point, he was spot on.

In fact, trees create weather. Through evapotranspiration, trees seed clouds with particles and water vapor that cause it to rain. Studies show that twice as much rain falls in the Amazon Basin than that which can be accounted for by showers coming in from the ocean. Consequently, as forests are removed, the Amazon area is becoming drier and less capable of growing trees.[13]

Over five hundred years after Columbus, scientists are discovering the complex and significant relationships between trees and the weather and affirming that deforestation influences climate across expansive landscapes. Accordingly, systematic tree conservation and restoration, particularly in coastal areas, can aid drought-stricken areas hundreds of miles away. And as is so often the case, human impacts on forests have the most profound effect on those who are most at risk.

Furthermore, scientists are beginning to appreciate not only that trees can help make rain and snow but also provide winds that move precipitation from the oceans further inland, the so-called biotic pump effect. The interior areas of Africa, South America, and other regions are reliant on both coastal and inland forests to pump much-needed precipitation to them from the rainy coast. The removal of coastal forests therefore plays a profound role in desertification, creating drought-ridden areas further inland and exacerbating the effects of climate change in many marginalized areas.[14]

This continuous process of transpiring water into the air and transporting rainfall over and over across continents creates "flying rivers." Amazingly, these rivers connect different continents, linking the weather patterns in the Amazon forest with those in west Africa and the weather patterns in the spruce forests of Alaska and northern

Canada with those in the Great Plains of the midwestern United States.[15] The weather that we have come to depend on in turn depends on forests.

The amazing capacity of the forests to make both wind and rain, to serve as both the lungs and the heartbeat of the planet, speaks to the astonishingly complex and critical relationships between forests and the well-being of the entire Earth.

Water on the Move

One of the most interesting aspects of water is that it is always on the move, traveling through the tree, the local watershed, and around the entire Earth, transforming itself into different forms—solid, liquid, and gas—as needed. When Robin Wall Kimmerer was struggling to learn the Ojibwe tongue of her ancestors, she found it particularly confusing when English nouns—such as days of the week and physical features—were verbs. When she was introduced to the verb *wiikwegamaa*, literally translated to English as "*to be* a bay" rather than just "a bay," she finally understood: "(T)o *be* a bay—releases the water from bondage and lets it live. 'To be a bay' holds the wonder that, for this moment, the living water has decided to shelter itself between these shores . . . Because it could do otherwise—become a stream or an ocean or a waterfall."[16]

While we all learned about the water cycle in grade school and might therefore take it for granted, the way water circulates around the globe is utterly fascinating and warrants another look. The movement of water around the planet connects species, landscapes, continents, and even time.

Water droplets from precipitation gather at the heights of mountains into small rivulets, which join other small channels to become streams. Streams combine into rivers, gaining strength and power as they move toward the ocean. Surface water seeps into crevices in the ground and forms vast underground systems of groundwater, which trees tap into for their use. The drooping branches of trees, especially designed to intercept precipitation, also direct rainwater into tree roots.

Both groundwater and surface water eventually dump into deltas or bays and finally into the vast storehouses of the ocean. Driven by the heat of the sun, water then returns to the atmosphere by way of evaporation from both soil and water bodies as well as from transpiration from plants and trees. When enough moisture builds up in the atmosphere, water condenses into clouds and falls back to Earth as rain and snow. During its life cycle, water is constantly being exchanged. Water that might be in the ocean one day is falling as rain somewhere else several days later.

The water cycle vividly demonstrates the interrelatedness and interdependence of all organisms and the deep connections between them. What affects the air affects the rivers. What affects the rivers affects the groundwater. What affects the groundwater affects the trees. What happens upstream affects life downstream. In and through the water, trees, birds, insects, fish, protozoa, worms, and all other living things are interconnected, interdependent, and enlivened by a Source known to, and experienced by, our spiritual ancestors for generations. Water envelops Earth and all its beings in Oneness.

Perhaps the most profound aspect of water is that it connects not only across geography but also across time. Water is a closed system. Many of the water molecules that exist today could have been on Earth for millions of years. In that time, they have circulated around Earth, in and out of various species, transforming from liquid to solid to vapor and back again. The rushing water carrying salmon at Brooks Falls last summer might today be circulating through an African baobab tree. And those same molecules might have been present in the roots of the bodhi tree that inspired the Buddha over twenty-five hundred years ago.

David Suzuki brings this message home: "We are water—the oceans flow through our veins, and our cells are inflated by water, our metabolic reactions mediated in aqueous solution . . . As air is a sacred gas, so is water a sacred liquid that . . . ties us back in time to the very birthplace of all life."[17]

This is the nature of water in trees—to move, to lift, to connect, to absorb, to give life.

Leah and I both live within the Potomac River Watershed and receive our drinking water from there. Since our bodies are made up largely of Potomac River water, we are, in fact, the river itself. Everything it has touched touches us. Our bodies have moved through sycamore and silver maple roots, been swum in by bass and catfish, been drunk by a thirsty heron, served as a nursery to salamanders and frogs, and provided a home to countless water striders, beetles, dragonflies, turtles, and countless other creatures. We, too, are part of Oneness.

Bringing It Home: Spiritual Practice

Intention
To encounter water as the spiritual circulatory system of the forest and of Earth.

Description

Find a comfortable place to sit with your teacher tree. You might lean against her. As you look out into the woods, imagine a single droplet of water falling from the sky. Trace it in your mind through the water cycle described in this chapter. Picture it falling to the ground and being absorbed by the soil before you. Imagine your teacher's tiny root hairs picking it up, along with some nutrients, then follow it as it flows up the tree through the xylem. Watch it as it moves all the way up to the highest leaves, where it is absorbed and used as part of the process of photosynthesis. See it as it escapes from the leaf through transpiration and joins with clouds in the sky.

Picture the clouds floating over the mountains nearest you and watch the little waterdrop fall into a creek high in the hills. Follow it as it gathers with other drops to form creeks, then streams, then rivers as it moves downstream. See it being withdrawn from the river and moving through pipes, where it comes into your home and finds its way into your morning coffee or tea.

Imagine it residing in your body. Feel the waterdrop inside of you and moving through you. Feel the fish who have swum in this water, birds who have drunk from it, salamanders who have laid their eggs in it. Feel all the plants and animals who have drunk from this water, including your teacher tree. Reflect on your being part of the Oneness.

Now see the little drop leaving your house through the sewage or septic system, back into the river, into the bay, and finally into the ocean, where it joins millions of other drops. Watch her again as she evaporates from the ocean and moves back into the sky to rejoin the clouds and start her journey over.

Every time you take a drink of water, you might close your eyes and feel again all the beings that have moved through it and through you.

CHAPTER 6

EMBRACING LIGHT AND DARK

LEAH

While I am looking for something large, bright, and unmistakably holy, God slips something small, dark, and apparently negligible in my pocket.

—BARBARA BROWN TAYLOR,
LEARNING TO WALK IN THE DARK

The words *light* and *dark* may evoke contradictory feelings for many of us. We often speak of *light* as good, welcoming, and what we aspire to or reach for, while *darkness* is held in the negative, a condition to be overcome. At other times, we equate darkness with much needed rest, a fallow time, or an inward journey, as we note that creativity and life evolve out of darkness. Or perhaps we hold light and dark simply as different ways of seeing, without judgment or negativity. For hundreds of thousands of years before humans walked this Earth, trees grew, thrived, and died in a dance with day and night, summer and winter. Trees hold spiritual wisdom for us as we consider the possibilities held within light and dark.

George McVey smiled wanly as he introduced himself to our group of four. His look suggested that he'd been on the receiving end of questioning looks and lame jokes before. I will admit that his name is not one I would have expected of someone born and raised on the Navajo reservation in Canyon de Chelly. For twenty years, he has owned and operated a jeep tour company, guiding outsiders through his Dine' homeland in what is now considered northeastern Arizona.

For nearly five thousand years, people have lived in these sandstone, shale, and limestone canyons formed by ancient seas and shaped by erosion. Ruins of ancestral Puebloan villages are built into the cliffsides, and petroglyphs and pictographs line rock walls. These can be accessed only via invisible-to-the-outsider trails that meander through the deep sand, around protruding rocks, and through gushing streams that sometimes turn the canyon floor into a swollen, rushing river. As we bumped along in George's jeep, holding on to whatever we could grab to stay upright, a fellow passenger mentioned how easy it must be to lose one's way on a moonless night, as the high cliffs encompassing the canyon allow only a sliver of sky to illuminate the land. George quickly debunked this view of darkness in the eighty-four-thousand-acre canyon: "You can drop me anywhere in this canyon on any night, and I can find my way home. I've walked this land day and night since I was eight years old." Silently, we pondered an intimacy with land that does not depend on light, a way of seeing that embraces both light and dark.

Reaching for Light

The shape of a tree tells the story of her journey toward the light. It's not hard to understand why: light is the life force

of a tree. Sunlight captured by a tree's leaves or needles ini-
tiates the process of photosynthesis, which gives the tree
most of the nutrients she needs to survive. Light provides
the essential energy needed to take carbon dioxide from
the air and water from the ground to produce sugars that
nurture a tree.

Trees employ a variety of strategies to position themselves for maximum light and to avoid being crowded out
by their neighbors. For example, beeches, firs, and spruce
grow to great heights and may soak up 97 percent of the
sunlight within a forest.[1] On the other hand, some trees
like dogwoods, spicebushes, and redbuds live underneath
the canopy of larger trees. They must bloom early to reach
the light before the larger, languid oaks and tulip poplars
get around to producing the foliage that will shade out
these smaller species. *Pioneer species* such as red cedar,
yellow poplar, aspen, and black locust seek out disturbed
or damaged ecosystems. By being among the first to move
into a cleared area, they can enjoy the sun and grow taller
before other trees emerge.[2]

Individual trees react, respond, and adapt to the
amount and angle of the light received. We can see this
as we walk in the woods: twisting and turning branches
grow in all directions to find more light. Some trees bend
their branches around their kin to reach the sunlight. On
steep slopes, trees may harvest light by growing nearly
perpendicular to the land.

Individual branches are strategic light-seekers as well.
When trees are growing in full light, one often sees bigger
and longer branches on their southern sides, from where
most light is coming.[3] Trees put forth leaves in different
patterns to minimize shielding other leaves from the light

even as they ensure that they can feed themselves.[4] Even then, leaves alter their position to face as much available light as possible. For example, on the southern side of trees, leaves typically point downward to catch the light arriving from below; on the northern side, leaves extend horizontally to catch the light from above.[5] This pattern makes sense as we recall how the sun sweeps across the sky to slowly set in the southwest.

We might think that the loss of older shading trees would be beneficial for younger saplings. In fact, they may receive more light upon the loss of taller trees, but many smaller trees are not equipped to deal with it. In the absence of the older trees upon which they were leaning, the young ones sway freely in the wind, resulting in tiny tears in their trunks that will need to be strengthened if they are to thrive. With energy devoted to repair, it may take several years before the trees are able to grow taller toward the sunlight. That extra time can be a good thing, given that their young leaves have become used to low light and would be scorched if exposed to the hot sun too soon.[6] Over millennia, trees have experience in knowing when and how much light is needed for their well-being.

As we envision these various practices the trees demonstrate for leaning into, opening to, or searching for light that nourishes and enlivens, we can consider the implications for our own spiritual journey. We might reflect on how to emulate our woody elders by doing everything we can to live into the light by whatever name we use—God, Allah, Source, One, Divine Mystery, Unity. Our paths to living more fully alive and connected to the sacred light is seldom straightforward. Like the trees, we, too, are called to bend, stretch, adapt, and turn. Sometimes staying small and blooming earlier is exactly what we are called to do. At other times, we may be invited to stop pushing so hard and simply yield to what is. Trees remind us that waiting patiently for our time while others around us are blooming is a valid practice too.

It might seem that trees are always competing for that precious gift of light. However, trees are collaborators as well, often sharing so that others in the forest can have what they need to live. For example, birch trees shade out smaller fir trees growing nearby in the summer, limiting the capacity of the fir to photosynthesize and produce the nutrients they need to live. During the time they are shading the fir trees, birches send nutrients to them through the underground fungal web connecting the forest. The tables are turned in early spring, when the buds of the fir sprout new needles while the birch leaves have yet to push forth, and again in the fall, after birch leaves are no longer photosynthesizing. Then the fir becomes a source of sugar for itself and the birch.[7]

Within us is an innate longing to share the rich harvest of the light with others. Sometimes that may mean that we will need to get out of the way so that we are not shading them. Often it will mean sharing the resources we have access to that they do not. When we are planted in a privileged position with access to the light, the birch and fir remind us of the necessity of sharing the bounty we have received from our privileged place with community members who have less.

As we observe the patterns of trees, we might consider how to stretch toward the light. Our practice probably won't look exactly like that of a tree, physically shaping ourselves to reach toward the sun. It might generate a similar feeling, however, as we listen for the places within us that are longing for more light and adapt our spiritual practices to respond to that need. Deepening our engagement with our teacher tree as a spiritual friend and noting how she responds to the light can increase our awareness of what feeds and what hinders our own spiritual life. Sharpening our awareness in this way contributes to our lifelong journey of spiritual deepening.

Trees have honed a specific, fascinating practice to reach for the light. Their light-oriented growth, called *phototropism*, requires that plants elongate their cells on the side of the leaf farthest from the light. In other words, when trees need to find light, they must stretch more on their dark sides; growth happens in the places hidden from the light.[8]

To embrace the practice of trees, we might notice the places within us where the light seldom shines. We may long to look away from our shadows, to ignore the ways we feel least connected to the holy. Yet the trees would tell us that those are the very places to which we must attend, lovingly stretching into the pain, misunderstanding, grief, or confusion. The trees remind us that if we refrain from growing in those difficult, shadowy places, our journey toward the light will be constrained.

Yielding to Darkness

Fear or dread may arise when we consider exploring the dark. From a young age, we might have heard that danger lurks in darkness. Giant trees block sunlight from the forest floor and create a land of shadows. Fairy tales warn us that harm is waiting in such places: *Be careful on your way to Grandmother's house. Don't stray from the path*. It's easy for fear to worm its way into our worldview. Some religious traditions emphasize seeking the light, living in the light, or letting our light shine to blot out the darkness of the world.

Most of us in the dominant Western culture can arrange our lives so that we encounter very little natural darkness. Abundant electrical lighting in most homes and on streets where we live means that we seldom sit with or walk in deep darkness. Even when we have pulled our shades and turned off the last light for the night, tiny glows from electrical devices ensure that it is never totally dark in most homes. We have become so accustomed to a state of perpetual light, it may not even occur to us there might be a downside of living with continuous illumination.

We may find ourselves avoiding darkness in our spiritual lives as well. It might seem that if we explore the darkness, it will overtake us, ensnaring us in negative emotions. In darkness, we may lose our way. Yet as we discover more of the spiritual wisdom of trees, we can see that light and darkness are equally important for them—and for us.

Acorns will not develop into vibrant oaks in a pot near a continuously sunny kitchen window; they require the cold darkness of a winter underground to sprout forth. The young scruffy acorn we met in chapter 2 must sink into the soil so that she can develop deep taproots and eventually create complex and far-reaching root systems. Her roots will absorb water and minerals with the help of mycelial networks and provide stability for the tree she is to become. This relationship with dark soil provides the glue and the grist that support the ecological functioning of the tree. So too, our roots, nurtured by the sacred in the dark depth of our souls, help to sustain our lives amid the storms that assail us.

There's something to be said as well about lingering in the shadows. Moving too quickly to seize the light before we have begun to develop our gifts more fully may ultimately be less fruitful than waiting patiently until our calling is revealed. In threshold moments, we become clear that we are no longer able or invited to stay in "what has been," and we may long to step boldly into a new future. Yet sometimes Spirit invites us to linger in discernment on the threshold, waiting patiently until the future emerges more clearly and we are welcomed into collaboration with the holy.

When a young tree first breaks through the soil, her world may not be filled with sunshine, and that limited light might serve her well. When some saplings grow in full sunlight, they develop too quickly and lack the strength they need to become healthy, long-lasting trees. Growing slowly gives many trees, particularly oaks, a better chance to live a long and healthy life.[9] To guide and protect them, *mother trees* shade their young, thereby slowing their growth and enabling them to preserve their energy. In Germany, shade cast intentionally by the mother tree is known as *instructive shade*.[10] When the mother tree eventually falls, her sheltered children can then draw on their reserves to grow tall and healthy, taking their place in the light-filled canopy for a century or more.

It's not just in the early life of a tree that vital functions happen in the mystery of darkness. We know from previous chapters that much of the ongoing life of a tree occurs out of sight. Leaves transpire and call forth water and minerals to flow from the roots to fuel photosynthesis. Food is shared with the roots and, through them, with neighboring trees and plants. Cells are forming sapwood, branches are being pruned, insects are being evaded. It can be quite lively in the dark.

My first response to being asked by a neighbor, "What's happening with you?" is often a recitation of the activities of the day, a review of my calendar, or an explanation of a future event. But like the trees, the true essence of my life, the most enlivening part of who I am, is stirring and growing beneath the surface. Our spiritual journeys invite us to sink into the rich soil of the sacred within, among, and around us all. This involves cracking open the hard shell that we imagine will protect us from sorrow or loss, permitting our souls to grow and expand in the fertile darkness, and becoming ever more deeply rooted in sacred connections that enable heart and soul to flourish. Without time for our taproots to ground in darkness and expand into an extensive, well-connected root system, we cannot become the oak we are meant to be. The bloom of our soul and its gift to the world can be lost without the benefit of darkness.

Of course, the ebb and flow of dark and light is not only about day and night; changes are embedded within the cycle of seasons as Earth's axis tilts toward and then away from the sun. Let's consider winter, the darkest time of year. Days give way to allow the dazzling display of moon and stars to linger on the sky's center stage. With the fading light and dropping temperatures, deciduous trees stop making food. Chlorophyll breaks down in most leafy trees, often revealing colors that were already present in the leaf but were masked by the abundance of green pigment.[11]

Eventually severed from access to water, autumn leaves will wither and fall to the ground, where they will be stirred and rearranged by the wind. This leaf layer will thicken, gradually decompose, and mulch the floor of the woods. The boney arms of oak and sycamore will scratch patterns in the steely sky, their movement calling attention to a spectrum of grays and browns gone unnoticed amid summer's green coat. With no necessity to strive for the light, the trees can rest.[12]

Throughout the long, cold, and harsh winter months, deciduous trees go dormant and look for all the world as if they are dead. But at the end of most branches are tiny buds, sometimes less than one-half inch, that hold all the energy and all the sustenance, everything that is needed for the tree to flower, produce leaves, and spread her seeds in the spring. The buds are wrapped tightly to withstand the snow, ice, and bitterly cold temperatures. By withdrawing water from the buds before the start of winter, the tree has protected them from frost damage. It's hard to imagine that tiny green leaves and flowers are folded within. Deer, squirrels, turkeys, purple finches, and other animals find winter nourishment in these dense packets of potential. These preformed buds give the trees a head start when spring arrives, as they are ready to break forth quickly to claim the returning light.

By tuning into the length of the day, the buds help determine the best possible time to exert light-seeking energy to grow. The buds of beeches wait until it is light for at least thirteen hours a day before they start releasing leaves. Buds will also note any unexpected arrival of light. When a neighboring tree falls, this new occurrence of sun triggers buds to open, allowing the emergence of leaves that can avail themselves of this unexpected gift.[13]

During a recent gathering, I heard people speak the word that arose for them when they thought of darkness. The words flowed into the circle: *earth, soil, rest, unknown, womb, comfort, revelatory, respite, stillness, seeds, growing, lingering.* I felt the calm deepen in the circle as we acknowledged the wisdom of the dark. We feel it when we listen to the trees. We sense it when we sink into the dark and quiet depths of our souls. Like the trees, we long to rest as we await another season of growth.

But we forget.

In *Learning to Walk in the Dark*, author and professor of religion Barbara Brown Taylor shared an experience of being guided by two experienced cavers into the absolute darkness of vast underground caverns. With the support of her guides, she felt safe as she gained courage. Brown mused that perhaps her guides were like spiritual directors who listen with her for how Spirit is moving in her life. "We go to counselors when we want help getting out of caves. We go to directors when we are ready to be led farther in."[14]

The same could be said of our tree teacher. When we are ready to continue our inward journey, this soul friend is waiting to guide us, for trees know darkness intimately. We do too. The experience of darkness is not as foreign to us as we might imagine; it is woven into every being that originated in the cosmos, the seed, or the womb. Life begins in darkness. Darkness begats light. It may seem ironic that so often our spiritual journey invites us to return to darkness so that we might sink in rest, cease our constant striving, remember where we have come from, and rediscover the sacred invitation encoded in our heart and soul. The invitation is not to dwell permanently in the cave of darkness but to summon the courage to sit without light so that we might glimpse the sacred beyond sight.

Light and darkness. Everything belongs.

Living In Between

While we often think of light and dark as the two times of day, there's another very important time in the forest. It is that in-between time we call dawn or dusk. In the evening, as the forest slows its light absorption to prepare for darkness, a variety of forest creatures are particularly active—moths and beetles, many birds and bats, skunks, deer, bobcats, and rabbits. Scientists refer to this twilight time as *crepuscular*. Crepuscular creatures find these times to be safer, as predators cannot see them as well in this in-between time. Spiritual teachers might call this *liminal* space.

Liminal comes from the Latin word *limin*, meaning "threshold." Liminal space or time finds us on a precipice or in a doorway, between old and new, past and present, light and dark, not fully in either place. Neither bathed in full light nor resting in darkness, we may find ourselves feeling confused or off balance in these in-between moments. Yet our human spiritual teachers speak often of this in-between time as offering particularly rich, if challenging, opportunities for spiritual deepening. And increasing our attention in liminal space can be an important spiritual practice.

I was presented with the opportunity to spend time in liminal space at a small family retreat center in the Shenandoah Valley of Virginia. Our host, Marie, invited us to join her for her practice of climbing a nearby hillside to watch the sunrise. My first question was, "What time does the sun come up?" It turns out that was not a useful question, as Marie's practice was to observe for hours as the sky moved from the depth of night to fullness of daylight.

Layered in most of the clothes I'd brought with me to ward off the night chill, I gathered with other sleepy retreatants in the lobby, where Marie supplied each of us with a thermos of coffee and an armful of blankets. The hill was steep and the air crisp, but the path was clear, and the stars shone brightly in a sky unhampered by artificial light. Wooden Adirondack chairs were already positioned at the hilltop facing east, even though the sky gave no hits of what was to come. After a few minutes of settling in, silence descended over our small group, and we were embraced by the night and the responsibility of keeping watch.

Without conversation to distract me, my senses grew sharper. I was able to be simply present to what was. After immeasurable time, the stars gradually gave their light to the sky and very slowly faded into the background to wait unseen for another day. Long before the sun began to rise, birds and animals stirred and exchanged acknowledgment of its coming. The shapes of distant trees began to emerge, first as a group, then as singular images. Geese flew overhead, their harsh calls announcing a new start as the sun's rays broke over the mountain, painting another original image as has been her practice for much of 4.5 billion years. There was darkness. There was light. And there was a time in between that I found difficult to describe. We could not return to what was. The day that lay before us was unknown. This liminal space was not simply marking time for what was to come; time in between held its own unique beauty and special wisdom.

For us, the trees, and Earth, these are liminal times. The ground is shifting beneath our feet culturally, ecologically, physically, and spiritually. Many of the stories that once guided us have lost their truth and luminosity; new ones are not yet formed to take their place. We can draw on the older, deeper wisdom of trees who have lived through times of great darkness, light, and the spaces in between to guide us as we wait on the threshold between times.

Embracing Light and Dark

The Cherokee people tell a story of the early days on Earth when the people longed only and always for the gift of light. Believing that they could never have too much light, people begged Creator: eliminate night and give us only daytime. Creator loved them and, although reluctant, granted their request. Before long, weeds grew with abandon, days were uncomfortably hot, and there was no time for rest. Soon the people realized the error of their ways. Again, they called upon Creator. With a newly acquired understanding of the importance of night, they asked for eternal darkness. Earth grew cold, crops failed, famine spread through the villages, and many people died.

Again, the people beseeched Creator: return the cycle of day and night as it was in the beginning of time. Creator heard their cries and reestablished the balance of light and dark. Filled with sorrow at the loss of so many people, Creator placed within the cedar tree the spirits of those who had been lost. When we smell the aroma of the sacred cedar or see her in the forest, we are invited to remember need for both light and dark and the losses we face when we do not honor them both.[15]

Trees show us how to grow toward the life-giving light, stretching on our dark sides to reach further, collaborating and sharing with others in community so that all might thrive. Trees know the importance of darkness, when they can droop and rest, when seeds are cracking open and deeply rooting. They understand in-between times of dawn and dusk, patiently watching for days to lengthen or grow shorter. We live within the rhythms of Earth and soul.

Like George, who knows the way home through the deep canyon in both light and dark, we, too, must chart our path in sunshine and shadow, drawing on the wisdom of trees to guide us.

Bringing It Home: Spiritual Practice

Intention
To experience a variety of times of light, dark, and in between in the woods and see the spiritual wisdom throughout the full range of light.

Description
Visit your tree teacher at different times of day and in differing amounts of light. Consider times of bright sunlight, diffuse light, light obscured by clouds or fog, dawn, dusk, and deep nighttime.

As usual, slow your breathing and your steps as you move into this sacred space. Tune yourself to deep listening. Take a blanket or chair so that you might sit with the tree, lean against her, or lie down under her crown.

Gaze around, seeing what comes to you. Notice how your teacher has responded to the light, the darkness, or the in between, or liminal, times. Notice how other forest creatures and plants are responding as well.

Now try to let all thoughts go and allow yourself to sink into and be enveloped by the light or the dark in whatever form it presents itself. Take the time you need to be present in this space. Note any feelings that come up with different types of light. See if questions arise about which you might want to journal or further reflect.

CHAPTER 7

IT'S ALL CONNECTED

LEAH

If we are missing the generosity and cooperation in the greater world, we are likely also missing these harmonious connections in ourselves.
—KRISTIN OHLSON, *SWEET IN TOOTH AND CLAW*

The roots of coast redwoods have a practice of what seems like holding hands. Growing in proximity to each other along the Pacific coast from central California to southern Oregon, they collect moisture from the fog that rolls in each morning. This location, however, leaves them vulnerable to fierce ocean storms. One might think that coast redwoods would have developed deep taproots to support their incredible height and anchor them securely in place; in fact, they have very shallow root systems. These giants remain standing through wind and rain because their roots are intertwined in a collective underground network that helps to stabilize all the trees in the forest. It turns out that trees have a rich history of collaborating for mutual benefit.

Trees as Collaborators

Arguably one of the most intriguing stories of trees collaborating is based on research from the Canadian scientist Suzanne Simard. Growing up in a family of loggers in the rainforests of British Columbia, she developed a love for, and understanding of, the forest community at an early age. As a young adult, she went to work for a logging company that aggressively clear-cut swaths of forest to create managed monocultures in tree plantations. The industry practice was to remove unmarketable species, thereby eliminating competition for light and resources in hopes of achieving more vigorous growth of the trees that produced useful lumber.

For example, paper birch trees were systematically cut down to improve the growth of the much more valuable Douglas fir trees. Yet despite the advantages the industry tried to create for the young fir trees, Simard observed that they were not strong and healthy. This puzzle led her on a journey of observation, trial and error, and ultimately rigorous scientific research to explore what the trees needed to thrive.

Simard set up an experiment to see if birch might have been supporting the fir trees in some way. Simard found that, as discussed in an earlier chapter, birch and fir growing in proximity to each other were not only trading photosynthetic carbon back and forth through an underground network, but they were also managing the exchange based on their changing needs. When the leaves of the birch shaded the smaller fir in the summer, the birch sent carbon to the fir. When the birch dropped her leaves in the fall, the fir transferred carbon to the leafless birch.

In Simard's words, the trees were working together like "an intelligent system, perceptive and responsive."[1]

This intelligent system encompasses more than the trees. An underground network of mycorrhizal fungi connects their roots. The fungi explore, scavenge, and salvage nutrients from rocks and soil and then offer the nutrients and water to plants in exchange for sugars, creating a system beneficial to all. In a naturally occurring forest, some hub trees—Simard dubbed them *Mother Trees*—may be connected via a *wood wide web* to as many as 250 or more other trees in a vast collaborative.

The story of collaboration is not unique to birch and fir. Similar exchanges occur in undisturbed beech forests, where trees feed each other to keep weaker trees alive. Trees even a few yards apart may experience different soil and water conditions and therefore would be expected to photosynthesize at a different rate. Yet studies have found that is not the case. Resources are redistributed between stronger and weaker trees by the underground fungal network so that trees with fewer resources still grow and thrive, benefiting from collaboration.[2]

Trees seem to understand that eliminating all competition is not good for the collective. Forester Peter Wohlleben noted that a beech forest is more productive when the trees are packed tightly together. If weaker trees are removed to increase the opportunity for more light to reach other trees, it opens the forest to wind and weather. Without a closed-loop system to which even the weaker trees contribute, the cool, moist climate is disrupted. Then all trees are weakened and become more susceptible to insect attack.[3]

This wood wide web of trees and fungi is so critical to the health of the entire forest that seeds just beginning to sprout in the mulch of the forest floor drop a chemical into the soil through their roots to invite the fungi to connect. When linked into the forest network, seedlings grow at a much higher rate than those growing without connections. Even when shaded by much larger trees that make getting enough light to photosynthesize a challenge, the networked seedlings are still at an advantage, presumably because they receive extra carbon sent to them from mother trees.[4]

It is impossible to know who's calling the shots in this web of collaboration: Does the fungal network direct the sharing process, creating stable conditions by ensuring that one tree species doesn't dominate?[5] Or do trees create a reciprocal relationship that balances competition with collaboration to support overall forest health?[6] Perhaps the relationships between the beings of the forest have been so deeply intertwined for so many millions of years that we will never be able to tease apart the whole. What we might say with some confidence is that the forest is a vast, diverse, and complex web wherein lives are intertwined and often thrive in collaboration and connection.

Of course, not all exchanges among trees are happening underground; there's plenty of action in the leaves of the upper canopy. By emitting volatile oils from their leaves, trees announce when they are under attacks by insects. These alerts are received by neighboring trees, which then produce their own chemical responses to hinder or repel insects.[7] On the African savanna, thorn acacias subjected to assault from giraffes produce a gas that signals to neighboring trees to mount their defenses. With the whole area of trees emitting toxic fumes, peckish giraffes must move upwind or wander farther away before they can resume snacking on tasty acacia leaves.[8]

Sometimes the defenses that trees can mount are not sufficient to save them; then they engage a different approach to meet the needs of the community. In chapter 3, Beth introduced you to biologist, educator, and writer Meg Lowman, who has spent most of her life studying tree canopies around the world. Lowman noted a frequent response from eucalyptus and tropical trees that have been devastated by insect attack or disease: "When adults were stressed and close to mortality, they oftentimes flowered and fruited profusely, as a last-ditch parental effort to propagate their genes into the next generation."[9] She was able to predict those trees that were dying because of their abnormally abundant flowering. It seemed that trees sometimes dedicated their remaining life energies to perpetuate their species and maintain the forest.

The Need for Connection

"There is something profoundly wrong with a solitary pine," author Ben Rawlence wrote. Rawlence traveled from Scotland, Norway, and Siberia to Alaska, Canada, and Greenland to study the health of the boreal forests. In his book *Treeline*, he wrote of the social nature of Scots pines, which share resources through underground fungal networks. Pines can live six or seven hundred years in a healthy forest where older pines send support to young saplings. At some point, the process reverses, and the mature trees in turn send nutrients to the aging pines. Sadly, but unsurprisingly, lone pines die much earlier than those in a forest. Indigenous peoples shared stories of solitary pines who whispered to humans of their loneliness and asked for companions to be planted nearby.[10]

Given all the ways trees depend on each other for well-being, we, too, might sense the need for kinship being whispered among the trees we have come to know. Trees suffer without relationships. So do we. The dominate Western culture often lauds self-reliance and independence. A guide for foreigners coming to the United States noted that most Americans are trained from early childhood to consider themselves as separate individuals, responsible for their own lives and livelihoods, and not as members of families or groups.[11] But if we think that we humans were designed to "go it alone," the trees are inviting us to rethink our assumption.

From all that we know about trees, we understand that no being is entirely self-made or self-sufficient. In millions of years of evolution, trees have grown in connection with each other and the systems that support them. In multiple examples, they demonstrate not only competition but also collaboration and reciprocity. Perhaps because we have failed to heed the wisdom of trees, we have forgotten that deep connections are necessary for the well-being of human bodies, hearts, and souls.

The COVID-19 pandemic demonstrated dramatically and perilously the power of and need for human connection. Yet even before that challenging time, Surgeon General Vivek Murthy had warned of an epidemic of loneliness in America.[12] Lack of social connection impacts our health, increasing the risk of heart disease and stroke and potentially increasing the risk for premature death as much as smoking up to fifteen cigarettes a day does.

Additionally, loneliness is associated with higher risk for anxiety, depression, and dementia.[13]

In 2023, the US Surgeon General's Advisory on the Healing Effects of Social Connection and Community produced a report that included this reminder: "Social connection is a fundamental human need, as essential to survival as food, water, and shelter. Throughout history, our ability to rely on one another has been crucial to survival. Now, even in modern times, we human beings are biologically wired for social connection."[14]

Although solitude plays an important role in one's spiritual journey, so do deep connections to others. Whether we acknowledge it or not, our well-being is deeply intertwined with that of our neighbors. Attempting to thrive on a lifetime focused on competition or isolation conflicts with the lessons of the trees—and everything we know about coming home to our souls. So often, though, those intimate connections seem beyond our reach. They may require both intention and attention.

We also have an innate longing to recognize our connections to the living world around us. Whether we remember or not, we are members of the larger sacred community, living in kinship with other beings. If we separate ourselves from that community, we suffer from what writer Michael Vincent McGinnis termed *species loneliness*, and we yearn to "re-establish and restore an ecology of shared identity."[15] The spiritual wisdom of trees may help us to remember the importance of having rich and vibrant connections to the sacred in all her forms.

Listening recently to a group of individuals reflect on places to which they felt most deeply connected, I noticed how many of them referenced their childhood. Julie spoke movingly of growing up on an island populated by summer residents. When autumn came, only her family remained behind. Left to her own devices, Julie roamed the land and studied the local flora and fauna in the serious way that children do. She explored the woods with abandon and found nooks where she could hide away. As she shared her memories, Julie observed with a tinge of sadness that she would never know another place as well as this once-familiar landscape. She noted, "If I needed to survive on my own without other humans, this would be the place where I could do that."

Half a continent away from Julie's island, Bill would have been packing his peanut butter sandwich in the early morning light of summer and then heading off on his bike, pedaling slowly so that his small but scrappy dog could keep pace. The creek outside of town was their playground and their laboratory. They explored where the spring bubbled forth from the ground to carve a twisting, turning creek bed lined with cottonwoods. Here Bill and his faithful companion could wade among the minnows that hid in the tree roots. Rocks and salamanders vied for their attention. It was not until the sun approached the distant hill that they would head back home for dinner, leaving their special space behind until the next day's adventure.

As he visited his grandparents, Jeff created memories among the giant elms that grew along both sides of their street and formed a vaulted cathedral for the vehicles that occasionally passed. It was among the large roots protruding from the ground that Jeff found contentment playing as a small child, the fascinating shapes engaging his imagination.

Julie, Bill, and Jeff were often without human companions, yet none of them recalled feeling lonely. They were deeply connected to the living world around them, and their relationships were abundant. They were not species lonely, for they learned early on that there is life-giving nourishment in connecting to the larger world to which we all belong.

"Our lack of intimacy with each other is in direct proportion to our lack of intimacy with the land,"[16] wrote Utah author Terry Tempest Williams. It is indeed a gift to have cultivated intimacy with the natural world in childhood. But even if that opportunity passed us by or if we have forgotten our connections, we can remember that we have never been truly disconnected. It is impossible to separate ourselves from the air we breathe, the water that gives us life, and the plants that feed our cells. At any time, we may choose to remember the ever-present kinship of beings held within the sacred web of life.

Deepening our intimacy with and connection to the trees can help to banish species loneliness. And this practice opens our hearts more fully to all of life. With open hearts, we are drawn into greater understanding, kinship, empathy, and compassion for lives unlike our own. Such deep connections to the lives of others comes at a cost. When compassion arises in us, not only do we long to relieve the suffering of others, but we also suffer along with them. We come to realize that we cannot enjoy well-being for ourselves until others do as well.

Beth writes about her experience with two young girls who experienced such compassion as they connected deeply and personally with animals in the forest:

> Our meeting place was about one hundred yards from the Potomac River and fifty yards off the main trail, nestled in an eastern deciduous forest where white oaks,

American beech, and red maples formed the "walls" of our church. For over a year, the Church of the Wild (now Wild Earth Spiritual Community) had gathered at this recreation area just outside Washington, DC, to explore the mutual indwelling of the Divine with the Earth and all its beings.

Thirty people showed up on a blistering July day—old and young, Black and white, individuals, couples, families. Undeterred by hot, sticky weather and the abundance of the insect members of our community who were present, we welcomed the spirits of those humans who had walked this area long before we had. We asked this broken land and all its creatures to gather with us, to teach us our right place in the great web. We held silence—lots and lots of silence.

Halfway through the gathering, I led a short reflection. A fallen ash log served as an altar in the middle of our circle, and I asked the group to picture a chipmunk sitting on the log; he was about six inches high, brown striped with a white belly, happily chewing on a pignut hickory nut. Then I asked the community to imagine that a bushy-tailed, tawny-coated predator had crept to the edge of the circle—a red fox, standing deathly still, eyes locked on the chipmunk as it continued relishing his treat, totally oblivious.

As we imagined the scene together, a little girl, maybe nine or ten, gasped. "Poor chipmunk," she sighed. "He's going to be eaten!"

From the opposite side of the circle, a girl about the same age replied, "But what about the fox? Maybe she's hungry. Maybe she has babies to feed."

I continued: "The fox just moved slightly, and the chipmunk is now aware of her presence. He drops the nut, jumps off the log and runs out of the circle. The fox is close behind. Do you see them?" The wide-eyed girls followed my finger as I traced the route of the imaginary chase. "Look! The chipmunk has spied the red oak. He takes a giant leap, grabs onto its bark, and scurries up the tree to safety. He looks down at the fox as she slumps slowly away."

"Whew! That's a relief," the first girl said.

"But now the fox and her babies will be hungry," the other responded.

Much has been made of the fact that human creatures have evolved an exceptional set of skills and abilities that have brought the world to the brink. Yet what about our ability—our gift—to feel empathy beyond our kinship group, indeed beyond our species? To see and sense both the chipmunk and the fox, and to imagine, to the extent we can, their experiences of the landscape we share? What about this gift of viewing the world through eyes that are not our own?

Could such compassion renew and enliven the forest around us that has generously offered its fellowship to us? The questions hovered as our community moved into a time of silent wandering and reflection.[17]

Fitting with the Forest

Trees are dependent not only on each other and their intimate relationships with the fungal network, but they also have formed vital symbiotic relationships with other species throughout the ecosystems where they live. Examples abound of relationships between birds and trees. Birds build nests with sticks or tiny branches in the crook of a tree or secure their place in a hole or hollow. Berries, buds, flowers, and seeds provide food for them throughout their lives. Birds may carry seeds away from the mother tree, enabling these harbingers of the future to find richer soil and more light than might be available at the base of their mother tree. Some birds serve as pollinators for trees as they seek nourishment from their flowers. Pinyon pines rely on western pinyon jays to crack open their hard nuts and spread their seeds. In turn, these jays depend on the nuts of the pinyon pine to feed their young.[18]

A variety of trees provide food for birds, as they nourish ants, spiders, crickets, worms, beetles, and grasshoppers. Because they eat oak leaves that are nutritionally dense, caterpillars serve as a super food for young chickadees and other birds.[19] During their approximately sixteen-day nesting period, the adult chickadees must deliver six thousand to nine thousand caterpillars to their single nest of fledglings.[20] Given this huge need for caterpillars, it's fortunate that oaks support 934 species of caterpillars in the United States.[21]

Sloths, koalas, flying snakes, geckos, tree frogs, and opossums spend much of their time living and sometimes eating in the canopy and would be at risk without the trees. Some plants need trees to assist their climb toward sunlight; others need shelter from the intense sun. Some plants depend on trees for nutrients that they cannot make themselves. Cancer root, for example, cannot photosynthesize; it usually grows near the base of an oak, where it can dig its roots into the oak roots and borrow the nutrients it needs without harming the oak. Cancer root pays it forward by serving as food for the black bear and white-tailed deer and offering astringent and other medicinals for humans.

Of course, while insects are being nurtured by trees and thereby providing food for birds, it's necessary to control the number of critters munching on a set of leaves or boring into bark if the trees are to survive. Birds help to balance out the number of insects chomping away on trees. When given free rein, nature demonstrates her wisdom about the importance of collaboration, giving and receiving in reciprocity.

Examples of such mutualism have been documented by scientists for many years. Even so, the story of living systems built through collaboration sometimes has taken a back seat to a story that places competition as the prime force of nature. The well-known phrase in Tennyson's poem—*nature, red in tooth and claw*—is often quoted to illustrate the brutality of the natural world. It's heartening to read Kristin Ohlson's recent book, *Sweet in Tooth and Claw: Stories of Generosity and Cooperation in the Natural World*,[22] as a counterbalance to that poetic phrase of old.

Arguably, even more impactful to our culture may be another oft-quoted phrase—*survival of the fittest*—from Darwin's *On the Origin of Species*. But Darwin did not actually use the term *fittest* in the first four editions of his book; he wrote about the survival of the *fit*. The nineteenth-century philosopher, Herbert Spencer, developed the phrase *survival of the fittest* after reading *Origin* to describe his theory that competition and gradual extinction of the weak were necessary for progress. Not until the fifth edition of the book did Darwin include the term *fittest*, popularized by Spencer.[23]

Only four letters make a big difference in meaning: To be *fit* to your place. *Fit* to your community. As biologist and author of *Biomimicry: Innovation Inspired by Nature* Janine Benyus explained to Krista Tippett in a 2023 interview, Darwin "understood that organisms don't just move into a place; they co-create a place and then the place creates them, and then they create the place."[24] This is an important distinction. Many of the trees we've discussed are not solely dedicated to outcompeting others around them; instead, we see that they are also adapting to, cocreating with, and collaborating in community.

This also is an invitation to consider how *we* might become fit to the place in which we reside and the ecosystem that generously shares life with us each day, to reflect on how to become a fit cocreator, a collaborator with the trees in our yard and in forests around the world. As Krista Tippett was quick to respond, we "already live on a planet that knows how to do that."[25]

However, before we embark on such a collaboration, we will want to listen for wisdom tucked within our hearts and souls, wisdom that illuminates our truest calling and purpose in these times. We do not become fit to place by trying to become someone other than who we are but by cracking open our outer shells to reveal the gift of our truest self, our hidden wholeness. As we sit with our anam cara tree, we seek to slow our busy, problem-focused mind so that we might listen with an open heart for what is being conveyed to us beyond words. In this way, we may glimpse our unique invitation to collaborate with humans, trees, and other beings who are already working toward a community of mutual thriving. In this way, we become fit to community.

This is the spiritual wisdom that trees offer. Our teachers know that collaboration is critical to mutual thriving. Over and over, they call us to a practice of collaboration and connection—a practice of vital importance to us and to life on Earth.

It's *All* Connected

We've explored how trees collaborate through extended networks and how they contribute to the lives of other species. In chapter 3, Beth introduced you to the large black oak whose life she has been following for some years. You may recall the wide range of critters whom Beth has seen finding food and shelter with this old tree: blue jays, titmice, chickadees, three species of woodpeckers, white-throated and song sparrows, various warblers and hawks, an occasional bald eagle, squirrels and chipmunks, raccoons, foxes, voles, rabbits, deer, turkey, and black bear! And that's just above ground. In chapter 4, on soil, we read about the vast network of underground beings who interact with trees. It's indeed an extended community in our trees and forests.

And there's more. The gifts of trees extend well beyond the boundaries of the forest. It's not an overstatement to say that forests enable Earth herself to be the vibrant and life-giving planet that we know today. The amazing capacity of the forests to make both wind and rain, to serve as the lungs and the heartbeat of the planet, are examples of the astonishingly complex and critical relationships between forests and the entire Earth.

In addition to being essential participants in the water cycle, trees are also key to a healthy, stable carbon cycle and the regulation of Earth's climate. Most of us remember learning in school that trees pull in carbon from the atmosphere, bind it in sugar during photosynthesis, and give off oxygen. Then the carbon is stored within the living tree and soil. Having perfected this process over hundreds of millions of years, forests are incredibly effective at carbon sequestration. The carbon capture capacity of trees along with the release of water vapor and aerosols help to cool the average global temperature by more than thirty-three degrees Fahrenheit.[26] It's noteworthy that every scenario offered by the Intergovernmental Panel on Climate Change that might help to limit global warming to sustainable levels involves reversing deforestation by 2030.[27]

Trees are also busy cleaning, sprucing up the air (pun intended), and generally improving the health of other living beings. For example, twenty-one to twenty-five medicinal biochemicals are concentrated in the growing tips and the resinous gum of spruce trees. These join with other spruce aerosols and are swept away on the wind to disinfect the airways for hundreds of thousands of miles.[28] Not to be left out, deciduous trees, especially maples, have special hairs on the underside of their leaves that comb particles out of the air, which are then flushed to the ground in the rains.[29] This is one more way that trees regularly gift the entire planet with fresh air.

Leaves that blanket the forest floor each autumn are another important benefit provided by the forests. Mature oaks offer some of the most nutritious leaf litter because their leaves decay very slowly. Oak litter improves water infiltration, helps retain moisture in the ground, harbors spring ephemerals, suppresses the growth of invasive species, and nurtures a diverse and abundant community of decomposers numbering in the millions under a single tree.[30] Nutrients created by the trees through photosynthesis are recycled by decomposers and returned to the trees and their progeny. Every component of the life cycle of a tree is important to the whole of the forest, and nothing is wasted.

Beth shared how salmon in Alaska, aided by brown bears, provide essential nutrients to the white spruce and western hemlock. Gifts from the ocean and rivers feed the trees—and trees return the favor. Tiny single-celled organisms—diatoms and desmids that make up the mass of phytoplankton, the base of the ocean food web—need nutrients and minerals to photosynthesize and divide. They receive these life-giving gifts as estuaries, coastlines, and deltas draw the nutrients of trees into the waters offshore.[31] These tree nutrients help to lay the foundation of the food web in the ocean and enable algae to photosynthesize. Continuing the gift cycle, algae in turn serve as a vital source of oxygen for this planet and all of us who live here.

Forests show us by example that separation is an illusion. When we look at eighty acres of ancient quaking aspen in Utah, the balsam poplar forest of Canada, or the stand of pawpaws outside my door in West Virginia, our eyes can deceive us. We see what looks like many individual trees but cannot see what links the many as one: identical DNA and one vast root system. These trees are a metaphor for oneness. Yet whether the trees we see are a single organism or many, the web of connection among all life is so extensive that surely the *inescapable network of mutuality* that Rev. Dr. Martin Luther King Jr. wrote about must apply not only to people but also to *all* beings on Earth.[32]

Reflecting on the many complex and beautiful tapestries of life supporting life can leave us amazed and deeply grateful. All of us are woven into this community, participants in this holy communion. Our bodies contain the very water of Earth, our cells are nourished by the photosynthesis of plants and the richness of soil, and the air we breathe is a gift of the forests.

Like trees, we are already and always in relationship, kin with all on this planet. The facts regarding the community of forests are amazing and wonderful. Yet as we sharpen our senses, we may find that we need not depend on facts, a comprehensive understanding, or even words to feel connection. We need only to open our hearts to become more fully aware of the sacred oneness of the living world. Lest we forget, our tree elders in the school of the forest stand ready and available to remind us.

Within each of us is harbored a deep awareness that all life exists in communion.

Bringing It Home: Spiritual Practice

Intention

To connect deeply with a tree and sense how it is collaborating with us and other beings. To open to the possibility of all life as sacred communion.

Description

Return to the tree who is teaching you. Remain in silence for a few minutes, allowing your mind to quiet. One by one, allow your senses to sharpen. Take in the tree and her surroundings. Look and listen for the connections between the tree and other trees. Do you see ways the tree is sharing with others around her? Through her roots? In the canopy? Do you notice other mammals, amphibians, reptiles, insects, or birds interacting with the tree? Stay still and open.

Then close your eyes and imagine what is happening beyond your view. Below ground. In the canopy. Inside the trunk. In your mind's eye, create a picture of connections and collaborations to visualize the networks. See the connections between the tree and you.

After an extended time, let go of visualizing, let go of words. Lean or lie back, eyes closed or gazing softly, and give permission for this web of sacred communion to enfold you. Stay in this space of open receptivity for as long as seems right for you and then journal or sketch about your experience.

CHAPTER 8

HOLDING LOSS, BEARING WITNESS

LEAH

The forest is part of our family. When we look at the forest, we don't just see forest. We see lives. Lives that need us just like we need them.

—KENAMPA, UNION OF INDIGENOUS PEOPLES, JAVARI VALLEY, IN JOHN W. REID AND THOMAS E. LOVEJOY'S *EVER GREEN*

I came to a full stop in the middle of my daily walk as I tried to absorb the tableau before me. I have seen trees split by lightning and quite a few that were blown over when their roots could no longer hold on against rain and wind. I've watched trees slowly give way to insects one limb at a time. I had never seen a tree fold in half, crown to roots, as if to touch her toes. The final shredding of her heartwood must have occurred at night, for no stories were circulated in our community about how this once-tall tree gave up standing and bowed to the ground. Her look of total surrender evoked a sadness deeper than I would have thought possible, given that I had only a nodding acquaintance with this oak. Loss can creep slowly or flounce boldly into life. I'd barely stopped to acknowledge this tree before; now I found myself mourning her.

The nearby vegetable garden held almost no signs of summer's vibrancy. Tender leaves had met their match in the morning frost; shriveled and crisp, they hung by a thread or stirred on the ground, awaiting final dissolving into new soil. Straw-covered beds encouraged the land to rest. Leaves, trunks, plants, and grass were painted from a palette of browns. Ironically, only one splattering of lively green remained—in the leaves of the folded tree, where her canopy, as if in final tribute, kissed the ground.

As we get to know trees, forests, and their ecosystems, we are often drawn more deeply into the beauty and wonder of it all. Yet as we deepen our awareness of and relationship with the woods near us, following the changing patterns of bark and leaves, we discover that loss is also present. The peace and healing that emanates from the woods are easy for us to accept; our instincts often prompt us to turn away from what feels difficult. But if indeed our work is to deepen our connection to the living world and cultivate our spiritual capacity, then we are called to see with the eyes of the heart, fully and fiercely. The heart encourages our engagement in *a long, loving look at the real.*[1] In the practice we call *bearing witness*, we face into all that is—joy, loss, beauty, grief—accepting and holding it all with deepening acknowledgment and compassion.

When we sustain an open-hearted gaze, accepting the pain that arises as our relationship with those who suffer deepens, we find ourselves more fully embracing and embraced within loving unity. Contemplative Martin Laird wrote that we enter the depths of the heart via a wound.[2] All hearts are wounded. It is our response to the wounds of life that makes the difference in our capacity become a more loving, vibrant presence.

Heart rot. That's what claimed the oak and bent her in half. A fungus or pathogen entered through a wound and spread throughout her heartwood. I reflect on how infrequently I consider what's growing in my heart, attend to what I am nurturing with continued practice, or wonder what might be spreading within me unacknowledged and unchallenged. Surely compassion for ourselves and others might be a balm for our wounds.

Our journey of bearing witness must be both inward and outward. The pain and heartbreak are opportunities. As Joanna Macy wrote, unlocking our pain "reconnects us with the larger web of life."[3] Wounded, we may open more fully to the difficulties that others face. Claiming kinship and acknowledging soul connections with trees implies that we will stay present with them, protecting them as we are able and acknowledging when we cannot. We will be as steadfast in supporting trees as we are for other friends and family members. Companioning kin throughout difficult times and bearing witness to their loss is never easy. Yet in doing so, our compassionate heart expands, and connections grow stronger.

When we shelter our hearts in hopes of protecting ourselves from hurt, we block the paths to hope-filled action. Until we unblock our feelings, "our power of creative response will be crippled."[4] Opening to our hidden wholeness—the ever-present, but sometimes-covered-over connection to the all-encompassing Divine—enables us to hold far more than we ever knew was possible and expands possibilities beyond our current imagining. Surely, this must be an antidote to heart rot.

It may be comforting to remember that we need not face alone the grief that bearing witness can evoke. Spiritual companions can lighten our burdens by sharing with us in conversations, practices, rituals, or simple silence. Such companions may be human friends of many years, or we may turn to the trees for quiet understanding that enables us to become more deeply acquainted with our grief and hold it more tenderly. I am one among those, who I imagine are many, who have received comfort from sharing with trees. Gazing out my bedroom window as I recovered from surgery, I felt the pines acknowledging and helping to hold my pain and fear.

Tragically, trees have born witness to and have been unwilling participants in some of our most heinous acts and our collective shame. In *Black Faces, White Spaces*, author Carolyn Finney reminds us that places considered "natural" by many "are overlaid with histories, seen and unseen; geographies of fear that can make a 'natural' place in the United States suspect to an African American."[5]

The National Memorial for Peace and Justice in Montgomery, Alabama, memorializes more than forty-four hundred Black people who were killed in racial terror lynchings. Their names are engraved on some eight hundred steel monuments that stand in for the trees that bore witness to these heinous events. Each monument represents a county in the United States where a known lynching took place.[6] One of these counties is in the Eastern Panhandle of West Virginia, where I live. This legacy of hate and violence is in the woods nearby. Close to home. The trees cannot forget, nor should we.

Grieving the Loss of Trees

One of the most pernicious threats to trees today comes from invasive predators—insects, fungi, disease—brought from abroad and from whom our native trees often have limited resistance. One of the most devastating predators was the lethal fungus that wiped out nearly two hundred million acres of chestnuts, beautiful native trees that often grew to over one hundred feet tall and sixteen feet in diameter, with a lifespan that could extend for five hundred years. Over a century ago, chestnuts reigned over two hundred million acres of eastern woodlands from Maine to Florida, from the Piedmont plateau in the Carolinas west to the Ohio Valley. Numbering nearly four billion, these giants dominated the landscape and provided food, shelter, and wood for the people who lived among them.

Then the late 1800s brought a rapidly spreading chestnut blight. Within fifty years, these once-giant trees were reduced to an underground root system that produced only shrubs. Those shrubs, too, succumbed to blight before reaching maturity. Although the roots persevere, the American chestnut is now considered functionally extinct.[7]

Despite the extent of loss, not everyone has given up on the chestnut. Through research and restoration, the American Chestnut Foundation (TACF) is experimenting with the development of disease-resistant trees in hopes that one day, they may be able to restore the American chestnut to its native range.[8] TACF is educating future generations of conservation leaders as well so that the work can be carried on into the future.

More recently, invasive pests and diseases are impacting other native trees. Dutch elm disease, emerald ash borers, hemlock woolly adelgids, spotted lanternflies, and mountain pine and other varieties of beetles are a few examples of dangers that have arrived in North America; the ash, elm, hemlock, pine, and other trees are under attack. With neither sufficient time for trees to develop immunity to the insects nor any natural predators on this continent, trees from the boreal forest of Canada through Central America face an ongoing struggle for their lives, a struggle that millions of trees lose each year.

Adding to the challenges faced by trees, climate chaos is resulting in increasingly higher temperatures, less snowfall, and extended drought. With insufficient water, the trunks of trees are less flexible and cannot extrude pests from the bark as they did when they were healthy. Under stress, the capacity of trees to resist insect and fungal attacks diminishes significantly. When large swaths of trees die off, remaining trees are subjected to a loss of moisture in soil that had been protected by a tightly knit forest. Dryer soil weakens the remaining trees as well. The understory of ferns, mosses, spring ephemerals, and bushes that supported a variety of wildlife give way to weedier, more arid plants. Many of these replacement species are invasive and therefore do not support native insects, birds, or mammals who live within the woods.

If an old tree is removed from the forest, the loss echoes throughout the natural community. Many of the ancient ones have connections to hundreds of other trees. When they are removed, millions of organisms in the fungal network are deprived of key sources of nourishment. Species that once protected each other suffer without their companions. Birds, insects, and hosts of mammals lose critical shelter and food. Dead and dying trees stoke hotter-burning fires that can ravage forests. Trees once survived and thrived in the cooler fires that Indigenous peoples used to manage forest growth; now their descendants face an extended, more intense fire season that burns hotter and lasts longer.

To build relationships with trees, to know a tree as kin, to fall in love with a forest, is to become vulnerable to loss. Once we open our hearts to new ways of seeing, the drawbridge is down, and grief can gain entrance. The artifice that we've cultivated to set us apart from other species—to insist that we are separate, unique, or even superior to them—no longer makes sense. As our paradigm of separateness begins to crumble, we *feel* more deeply what happens to other beings. We might say that in cracking open, we become more authentically ourselves as members of the Earth family. Like a tree who demonstrates the paradox of being a single entity while deeply intertwined with multitudes, we are both individual and collective.

Psychologists warn that rapid changes to the planet are bringing about stress and mental anguish. *Ecoanxiety* and *ecogrief* are understandable and normal responses to what is happening to our beloved world. *Solastalgia* denotes a kind of "homesickness" where people remain in place, but their once-familiar ecosystem changes around them. A recent study by the American Psychological Association found that more than two-thirds of Americans reported at least some ecoanxiety. When the losses are both recurring and increasing in intensity, there is insufficient time for us to recover from one loss before we face another, even greater threat.[9] Loss is real and present.

As we noted earlier, loss is difficult to face—and loss offers an important opportunity for spiritual growth. Author and professor Belden C. Lane wrote: "The threat to *natural* wilderness forces us into the *inner* wilderness of the human psyche where wonder, grief, and longing are storming within us as well. Every experience in the natural world invites us to a corresponding work of the soul."[10] This work of the soul opens us more fully to the emotions of life—loss, delight, pain, wonder, sorrow, and joy. As our relationship with our tree teacher deepens, as we become fast soul friends, our love expands to encompass all beings.

Just as brokenness and loss are interwoven with wonder and beauty in a woodland, so too for us. In chapter 2, we wrote of the importance of beauty, awe, and wonder to our lives. When we are examining the exquisite detail of a tiny hemlock pine cone, gazing skyward to a majestic green canopy, or envisioning the vast complexity of the underground network of trees and fungi, we often find that our inner voices quiet and we lose our sense of a separate self as we are absorbed into the holy everything.

As we assume the responsibility of bearing witness to loss, claiming the beauty alongside—and even within—the loss offers solace for our wounded hearts. "Indeed, it is often the whispers and glimpses of beauty which enable people to endure on desperate frontiers. Even, and perhaps especially, in the bleakest times, we can still discover and awaken beauty; these are precisely the times when we need it most."[11] As beauty, awe, and wonder interweave with loss and grief in our lives, we may open ever more fully to the sacred wholeness within us, within all, and within which everything is held.

Expanding Our Love and Witness to the Forests

There are five megaforests on Earth: the Amazon, the Congo, the rainforest of New Guinea, the Taiga that is mostly in the boreal zone of Russia, and the North American boreal in Canada and Alaska. In *Ever Green*, economist John Reid and biologist Thomas Lovejoy wrote that because of the positive correlation between the amount of biodiversity and the amount of carbon stored by a forest, it is critical that we protect these five great forests to have a chance of keeping climate change within tolerable limits.[12] Of course, preserving biodiversity is at least as important as carbon sequestration, and these forests are home to a stunningly rich array of life. Alas, all is not well with these forests.

Logging, deforestation, mining, oil and gas pipelines, and an expanding system of roads threaten the boreal forests of Canada. In the provinces of Ontario and Quebec, an area of boreal forest approximately the size of New York state has been removed since 1976. Replanted forests hold less carbon, are more vulnerable to disease and insects, and provide significantly poorer habitats for plants and animals than the old-growth forests they replaced.[13] Additionally, the patchwork of trees left behind are more susceptible to forest fires. This was evident to many of us in 2023 when thick smoke of the burning boreal blanked Canada and the northern United States for many days. Approximately 18.5 million hectares (71,000 square miles) burned in those fires, far surpassing the previous record of 7.6 million hectares in 1989.[14]

In the Amazon, fires are deliberately set to clear vast stretches of forest for industrial-sized soy plantations to feed pigs and chickens. Other huge clearings are being transformed into scrubby rangelands for grazing cattle. Three of the largest grocery chains in the United States sell beef from a company linked to this practice—a practice that maximizes corporate profits and satisfies the desire for cheap beef while threatening the homelands of many Indigenous people.[15]

The challenges are similar in New Guinea and Indonesia, where forests face threats from farming, logging, gold and copper mining, and palm oil production.[16] Palm oil—used in toothpaste, ice cream, cakes, chocolate, cosmetics, soap, shampoo, cleaning products, and biofuel, to name just a few items—is now "the commodity consumed by Americans that contributes most to the loss of tropical forests."[17] Palm oil trees are grown on huge plantations that are built after biodiverse rainforests have been clearcut and burned.

The Congo is known for its rich, biodiverse megaforest and for the largest-in-the-world expanse of peatlands that cover over thirty-eight thousand square miles. Together these absorb carbon equivalent to ten years of global emissions.[18] In 2022, the president of the Democratic Republic of Congo (DRC) opened over twenty-seven million acres of Congo's forests to drilling for oil and methene gas. Meanwhile, in the enormous Russian taiga that stretches for more than three million square miles across two continents and ten time zones, the permafrost is melting, and fires rage in summer. Because the climate is warming, several tree species are expanding northward; sadly, their spread adds to the increasing temperatures as the sun-reflecting icy tundra is replaced with sun-absorbing trees.[19]

There is no way to skirt the issue; the consumer-focused lifestyle of much of the Western world threatens the lives of trees and forests. The losses continue to mount. And because these megaforests are intensely interconnected with vast ecological and earth systems, Earth is being harmed. As we noted in chapter 7, Earth depends on trees to maintain both water and carbon cycles, cool land and oceans, help make wind and rain, and provide oxygen needed for life. Without the great forests, climate chaos runs amok, and Earth's systems break down.

Importantly, each of these great old forests is home to Indigenous peoples who live within and care for the ecosystem, people who for generations beyond time have shaped the forest and been shaped by her. Although they comprise less than 5 percent of the world's population, Indigenous peoples protect 80 percent of global biodiversity.[20]

To many Indigenous peoples, the idea of nature as other-than-human is inconceivable. Professor and anthropologist Enrique Salmon termed this concept *kincentric ecology*—the worldview that embraces everything around us as our relatives.[21] As Casey Camp-Horinek, environmental ambassador and elder and hereditary drumkeeper from the Ponca tribe of Oklahoma, offered in her presentation at the 2024 Bioneers Conference, "We have to realize that we're not protecting nature. We are nature protecting itself."[22]

As we consider how the health of the world's forests is being jeopardized, we may feel that bearing witness is too much to ask. It may help us to remember that this spiritual practice has the capacity for healing both the receiver and the giver. As our hearts are broken open, we increase our capacity to hold more sorrow, beauty, loss, joy, grief, and love. Bound together as beings of the cosmos and recipients of these gifts of this living world, we are entangled forever in a web of love and loss. Bearing witness enables us to recognize that deep connection with the life-giving forests and to realize more fully the depth and richness of our love for all beings.

With forests under assault from large-scale logging, extraction, and farming projects, Indigenous and local people are on the front line, bearing witness to the losses and working to protect these lands. Fortunately, some governments around the world have begun recognizing the right of Indigenous peoples to manage the land and forests they know so well. In Namibia, a program of community-based natural resource management has resulted in the establishment of eighty-two conservancies and thirty-two community forests. Canada's Indigenous Guardianship program recognized the rights of Indigenous communities to manage their territories according to traditional laws. Australia recently extended support for Indigenous Protected Areas.[23]

In many forests, Indigenous people have organized to defend their homeland. Mujeres Amazónicas Defensoras de la Selva, a collective of women from seven nationalities of the Ecuadorian Amazon, advocate for the protection of their traditional lands, education, health, and women's rights.[24] The Women's Earth & Climate Action Network (WECAN) Itombwe forest program in the DRC works to define the rights of Indigenous forest-dwelling communities and elevate the leadership of women in protecting over 1.6 million acres of rainforest. This work involves "revitalizing Traditional Ecological Knowledge and cultural practices of reciprocity toward the forest."[25] These are only two examples of a multitude of Indigenous groups from around the world working for the protection of forests.

When we connect more deeply with the trees and forests, we also connect more deeply with the people who love them. As we become increasingly aware of the many times we have treated nature as "other than" us, we also may see that we have considered people with different practices, cultures, or even physical appearances as "other than" us. The spiritual wisdom of trees reminds us of the importance of reweaving our connections, bringing us back into collaboration and connection for the sake of our hearts' longing and the well-being of all.

Standing up against large corporate and governmental interests is dangerous work for the forest protectors and can result in harassment, threats to one's physical safety, disappearance, and even death.[26] The deep, open-hearted courage of these protectors offers inspiration, invites us to bear witness and grieve with them, and encourages us to stand in solidarity to protect these forests on which all life depends.

Taking It Personally

Old-growth forests speak to my soul. In 2019, my husband and I spent two weeks in California visiting Sequoia, Kings Canyon, and Yosemite National Parks. Although the tour guides throughout were well informed and engaging, we felt drawn to wander off on our own. I sought the chance to linger with, gaze upon, touch, and inhale these towering trees, for there's a space in my heart that only these trees can fill. Old-growth forests feel saturated with wisdom; tree teachers abound. We had driven by extensive burn areas before arriving at the park, but walking among a forest of such ancient immensity comprised of trees endowed with thick bark to protect from fire offered hope that *these* trees were beyond harm. Such was not the case.

The Castle Fire, which burned through California's Sierra Nevada in 2020, killed an estimated 7,500 to 10,600 sequoias with trunks more than four feet in diameter. More than 10 to 14 percent of the giant sequoias were lost across their natural range in the Sierra Nevada. Although the National Park Service acknowledged that it was not possible to be precise, it estimated that these giants may have ranged from hundreds to as much as two thousand to three thousand years old.[27]

These sequoias have coexisted with fire for thousands of years, their thick bark insulating them from the heat, their branches growing high enough to avoid most flames. Historically, low to moderate fires burned regularly in these groves, releasing seeds from sequoia cones and creating gaps where the seedlings could grow. Now fires are more severe, and these giant trees have been weakened by a warming climate. Six fires between 2015 and 2021 pushed the forests to a tipping point.[28] I weep for the tragic loss of these beautiful, ancient trees and all the beings who lived among them. I grieve for generations who will not know their grandeur. I am heartbroken for the many ways that Earth is poorer for their loss. Sometimes all I can do is simply be with the sadness.

I sat on a park bench in a cemetery near our home under the sheltering branches of a large red cedar. Of course, a cedar is nothing like a sequoia and could never replace the sense of being enveloped by life that I felt as I walked among the sequoias. Yet there stood the cedar, fully present in her "cedarness," literally and figuratively embracing me with her soft branches, helping to hold my sorrow in ways I still don't understand.

Some months later, our community gathered to plant over a hundred trees in a nearby conservation area. In groups of two to three, we knelt, carefully separating the roots of individual oak, maple, and evergreen saplings; placing each one into a hole; and covering the roots with soil to encourage them to form connections to the underground community. Somewhere in the midst of the planting, I became aware that I had been wrapped in a continuous prayer, a songline of dreams unfolding at the blurry edge beyond my knowing. Healing may come as an unexpected gift as we plant possibilities beyond our lifetime.

On our "trees trip," we also visited parks with magnificent redwoods. One of several such sites, Humboldt Redwoods State Park, harbors the largest remaining old-growth redwood forest in the world. Coast redwoods over two thousand years old live here. At a height of up to 370 feet, they hold the distinction of being the tallest trees on Earth. As we wandered among them, we learned that their bark holds tannic acids that retard flames. Given this gift of nature, I thought that surely coast redwoods would enjoy a wide margin of safety.

Then in August of 2020, lightning ignited fires around California's Big Basin Redwoods State Park. In this intense blaze, flames shot through the forest canopy, burned even the uppermost branches, and incinerated the needles that provided the means of photosynthesis. It seemed that all had been lost. Yet we can never truly know how the future will unfold.

Only a few months after the fire, fresh growth emerged from the blackened trunks. Foresters who worked among and knew these trees were surprised and delighted by the discovery of this new growth. Despite being defoliated, sugars made from sunlight decades earlier had been mobilized and sent to buds that were lying dormant in the bark for centuries.[29] Waiting for centuries.

There will be times, especially when we are at our most vulnerable, that we cannot hold all that arises as we bear witness. Then we may need to pause to catch our breath, recenter, and create space to remember and embrace the awe, wonder, and beauty that exists alongside the loss. This is not a recommendation to ignore losses but rather to enlarge our view to allow the mingling of grief and gratitude, loss, and wonder. Deep relationships are woven from a complex fabric of feelings. Taking a step back for a wider, longer view can enhance and enlarge our capacity for bearing witness. From that space, we can acknowledge that loss and joy can both be true and are often interwoven.

Our tree teachers have inherited and cultivated deep wisdom that has enabled them to live through hundreds of centuries of trials and difficulties. This is not to suggest that they can withstand every strike against them. The climate is changing more rapidly than ever, and living beings have limited time to adapt and evolve. With eyes wide open, we mourn the losses—past and impending—and we celebrate the unexpected ways that trees hold fast to life. Amid the loss, wonder is present. Within the loss, trees still surprise and inspire us.

What Is Mine to Do

Bearing witness isn't just about opening our eyes and heart to losses caused by others. It also requires that we look with courage and clarity at how we contribute to loss—intentionally or inadvertently—through our lifestyle and practices. We don't have control over everything; we do have control over some things, perhaps more than we like to admit. Acknowledging our culpability in the loss of trees is incredibly painful. But unless we look fully at the consequences of our actions, we cannot learn, seek forgiveness, or take actions to make amends.

The choices we make every day are impacting trees. We've already noted how soy plantations to feed pigs and chickens, pasture for beef cattle, and palm oil plantations are decimating forests around the world. Additionally, hundreds of thousands of tons of wood pulp that is used in the United States to make the most unsustainable brands of toilet paper, tissue, and paper towels come from the Canadian boreal forests. Most of the logging is done by clear-cutting. This process devastates the ecosystem and releases carbon from these forests that store more carbon per acre than any other biome on Earth. The Natural Resources Defense Council's latest "tissue score card" gives a sustainability grade of F to the major popular brands that you would surely recognize. It's instructive to note that these brands have not changed their practices nor improved their score since the rating system began five years ago, in 2019.[30]

I recently decided to take inventory of the trees that have been cut to support my current lifestyle. My husband and I live in a semidetached home of approximately nineteen hundred square feet, not particularly large by some American standards but more than sufficient for the two of us. Research reveals that an average semidetached home of 2,301 square feet—larger than our home but still in the ballpark—would require 102 to 117 trees. In my mind's eye, I imagined the felling of a hundred trees to build the home in which we live. So many. I was stunned. I had no idea how to calculate the added wood for interior doors, built-in cabinets, and engineered hardwood flooring. Our bedroom furniture is all wood, but we've had it for thirty years, so I felt a little better about that. Our living room furniture is upholstered around wooden frames. More trees. Our dining table and bench are made from fallen trees that were milled and handcrafted locally. Maybe not quite so bad? Still, I saw myself surrounded by the lives of former trees.

Add bookcases, books, desks, shelving, picture frames, printer paper, cardboard packing boxes, mailings, and catalogs—the list went on. We committed years ago to stop buying food and household products that are produced by clear-cutting forests. These efforts seem small in comparison to our ongoing use. So much wood for our lives. It was difficult for me to absorb the results of my personal survey. A variety of feelings and thoughts arose in me: shame, sadness, appreciation, amazement, gratitude, a longing for forgiveness, an urge to simplify my life, the importance of giving back.

Seeing with the eyes of the heart, taking that long, loving look at the real, was anything but a walk in the park when bearing witness to the loss of trees and my personal contributions. Bearing witness opened me to intense and unpleasant feelings to say the least. This practice also reminded me of the gifts of trees, my love for them, how much I still need to learn, and changes I am called to make.

Staying present to pain and sorrow *and* deepening our understanding, compassion, and wonder—all are part of the spiritual practice of bearing witness. We are woven into a vast cosmos and a local landscape. Earth calls us, over and over, to take our place in the *family* of things. With that very good medicine, over time we find that we are better able to behold moments of magic with tears in our eyes, to witness what once would have seemed unbearable while holding everything in deep love—as we, too, are held.

Everything belongs.

Bringing It Home: Spiritual Practice

Intention

To witness and hold in our hearts the ways trees bear great difficulties even as they maintain resilience. To allow trees to be our teachers as we seek to hold and participate in grief and loss along with awe and wonder.

Description

Return to your teacher tree. Begin by quieting any busy thoughts in your mind. Let go of thoughts that take you to the past or the future. Open to being present in each moment.

When you are ready, gaze upon this tree, looking softly, without judgment. See what is, just as it is. Notice where there may be wounds, past or present. As you gaze upon the wounds, intentionally keep opening your heart. See the wounds just as they are, noticing any feelings that come up. Simply name those feelings and breathe into them.

Ask the tree, "What's it like to be you?" Listen for her response. Then wonder with her: "Is there any way that I am contributing to your pain? Am I harming those around you? What do you need from me?"

Wait patiently for any answers that may be given, without trying to make anything happen.

Acknowledge the tree and thank her for sharing with you, just as you would acknowledge such sharing from a human friend. Then sketch, journal, walk slowly, or sit in silence, allowing a deeper awareness of this experience to arise from your heart.

Come back to open-hearted wondering about this experience throughout the next few weeks. Notice if there is any invitation for you.

CHAPTER 9

COMFORT, RESILIENCE, AND HEALING

BETH

Along some parts of the coast where there is a steady wind from the sea . . . it is extremely difficult for trees to grow tall and straight against the sky. Yet they do . . . It is a very fine art, this bending with the wind and keeping on.

—HOWARD THURMAN, *DEEP IS THE HUNGER*

We do not need to bear witness to and grieve the loss of our tree kin, or other losses we might suffer, by ourselves. Trees, who have shown extraordinary resilience in the face of extensive injury, are companions well suited to our journey through sorrow to healing.

Mutual Woundedness

A few years ago, on a chilly autumn day, I participated in a grief walk in a beautiful old hardwood forest. Members of the group had experienced a wide range of recent losses, including some that were devastating. As we began our introductions, I noticed one man standing off to the side by himself. His face was drawn. He was stooped, as if carrying a heavy sack on his shoulders. It seemed like an effort to hold his head up. I had learned earlier that this man's sixteen-year-old daughter had recently died by suicide. I could not imagine the depth of his loss.

Protected and enveloped by towering ramrod-straight tulip trees and huge shaggy white oaks, we walked slowly down the wooded path in silent single file until we reached the bottom of the valley, the belly of the forest. Some in the group gasped as they saw the huge sixty-feet-high, four-feet-wide tulip tree. About ten feet of the huge trunk had been culled out, and the enormous jagged wound stood open and exposed. It looked as if a giant ice-cream scooper had taken out the entire bottom of the tree. The heartwood was almost completely gone, and the tree was being held up on only three sides. Certainly, she was no longer living. Who could survive that kind of loss?

But when we looked up, we saw those telltale green tulip-shaped leaves scattered on her branches as far as we could see. Squirrels were skittering up and down her bark, and blue jays were pecking at her seeds. Her heart(wood) was gone, yet she survived. She would never be the same tree. She would always bear the scars of her loss. Yet she lived. And she was still giving back to others within the forest community.

I watched our group take in this noble, wounded survivor. Tentatively, the grieving father approached the tree. He reached inside the remaining tree bark and touched her ragged interior. He then spoke softly to her and walked away.

I will never know what this heartbroken father said to the tulip tree, nor the impact that visit had on him. I would like to think that, if only for a moment or two, he found some comfort. Perhaps the visible deep cuts within the tulip tree gave him a place to put his own horrific loss. Perhaps the tree reassured him that he, too, would learn to live again in his wounded state, despite the hole that would always remain in his heart.

I must confess that I, too, in moments of overwhelming loss, have spent time curled up inside that big old tree and have felt held and supported in my own grief.

What was it about this wounded giant that touched this grieving father, that made me want to crawl inside of her and be comforted? In his description of how he fell in love with Grandfather Tree, Belden C. Lane talks about how he was drawn to the tree because the extensive storm damage Grandfather had endured spoke to him as he was grieving the loss of his mother. "Suffering," Lane says, is "the door, joining us by a mutual woundedness."[1]

Quite possibly, it was mutual woundedness that drew the injured father, and me, to the injured tulip tree. As we connect intimately with a broken tree that still lives, still grows, and still gives back, we draw sustenance and hope that we, too, will somehow go on despite carrying seemingly unbearable pain. The tree does not offer us a superficial hope that life will be as it was before. Rather, she reminds us that we will somehow learn to live with our brokenness and, in time, live a full, if altered, life.

Trees for Life, a group that is dedicated to rewilding the Scottish Highlands, routinely brings refugees, the homeless, and those struggling with mental health issues to the Highlands for the arduous work of tree planting in a rugged and remote area. Through its Rewild and Recover program, people actively participate in the healing of the forest and are in turn healed in the process. Said one participant: "For me, it wasn't a holiday. It was emergency first aid on a completely crushed and flattened brain. I arrived virtually dysfunctional and at a dead stop . . . I have managed to get home in a functional state and standing upright again. . . . At least I'm back in a position where I can try and do something about it."[2]

When we broken and lost individuals connect intimately with a forest that is undergoing decay, disease, infestation, or complete devastation at the hand of aggressive logging, we experience a visceral soul-to-soul empathy with the trees. The health of all species within the forest is bound together in an inextricable web of belonging. Since we are now one, we cannot separate our human needs from those of our other-than-human kin. Our wounds do not cut quite as deeply, as they are now shared with other family members who have also known injury. By helping to heal the trees, then, we, too, are healed. As Buddhist ecoactivist Joanna Macy says, "As we work to heal the earth, the earth heals us."[3]

This mutual healing can manifest itself in communities as well. After a prolonged period of clear-cutting in Kenyan forests, poor villages no longer had adequate fuel for stoves or water for drinking and bathing, significantly disrupting community stability. The impact was particularly difficult for women, who had to walk farther and farther for wood and water. In response to this dire situation in her homeland, Nobel Prize–winning activist Wangari Maathai mobilized thousands of women to plant more than thirty million trees.[4] As the trees came back, more sustainable harvesting practices were put in place, clean water was more available, and economic opportunity and empowerment increased for women within the community structure.

Comfort

Most of us are familiar with the tragic story of Anne Frank, who along with her family and four others, hid from the Nazis for two years in a secret annex in Amsterdam. What might be less familiar is the role that a white chestnut tree outside a tiny attic window played in giving her comfort during this terrible time. Her father, Otto Frank, expressed his surprise when, in reading her diaries, he discovered how significant the tree was to her: "She longed for it when she felt like a bird in a cage. Only the thought of the freedom of nature gave her comfort."

And in her own words, she said: "The two of us looked out at the blue sky, the bare chestnut tree glistening with dew, the seagulls and other birds glinting with silver as they swooped through the air, and we were so moved and entranced we couldn't speak."[5]

In 2005, sixty years after Anne Frank's death and when it was clear the old tree was dying, hundreds of volunteers gathered its nuts and sent them around the world to honor Frank and her brave legacy. In 2014, a sapling from one of those nuts was planted on the US Capitol grounds to remind us of the resilience Frank demonstrated under unimaginable circumstances.[6]

This story of Anne Frank reminds me, too, of my friend Becky, whose disabilities have required her to live in a nursing home, where she is one of the youngest residents. Becky regularly sends pictures of her beloved locust, basswood, and other trees whom she sees out her window and on the grounds every day. She has told me how important the trees are to her as she feels stuck inside her circumstances with little hope for relief. In her loneliest moments, the trees keep her company and connected with a world far vaster than her small room.

Trees also held a particularly special place for the well-known theologian and mystic Howard Thurman. As a young Black boy growing up in northeast Florida early in the twentieth century, he often experienced the sting of racism. He would regularly go to the woods, where one particular oak tree would provide comfort: "I could sit my back against its trunk, and feel the same peace that would come to me in my bed at night. I could reach down in the quiet places of my spirit, take out my bruises and my joys, unfold them, and talk about them. I could talk aloud to the oak tree and know that I was understood."[7]

The therapeutic benefits of the natural world are now well documented, and the field of ecopsychology is flourishing. Florence Williams' comprehensive work, *The Nature Fix*, documents how time in nature calms anxiety, lowers our blood pressure, and even makes us more compassionate.[8] A recent study found that access to nature plays a significant role in the healing of the most severe hospital patients as well as contributing to the health of the medical staff.[9]

When we take in the twinkling yellow of hundreds of aspens on a Colorado mountainside or simply walk by a magnificent elm on a busy city street, we feel better. We take a breath. Perhaps we slow our gait. Or just look around and take it all in. Trees bring us outside of our contracted selves. They beckon us to look up and out. They take us outside of our day-to-day worries and into a broader landscape that provides much-needed perspective. They quiet the noisy voices inside of us. They move us and humble us.

During recent times of national and international crisis, record numbers of people went to the woods. There was something the trees gave them, whether they could articulate it or not—perhaps a sense of wonder, beauty, or awe; perhaps a sense of stability and predictability; or perhaps just a well-needed break in the midst of the chaos.

Something more is at play as well. Traveling within our DNA, within what ecopsychologists call our *ecounconscious*, there might well be the memory of our first home deep in the forest. Among the trees, long-forgotten memories awaken. While we are not often conscious of it, the sweet smell of pine, the various reds and golds of the maples, the rough touch of the bark of a Douglas fir, the shrill cry of the red-tailed hawk, or the savory taste of a morel mushroom might bring us back to a place that once provided everything we needed for food, water, and shelter. Here, too, connected to our earliest home, we not only know where we are, but we also know who we are—our first and most real self, unburdened by current expectations and anxieties.

For the last forty years, Japan has made *forest bathing*, or *shinrin-yoku*, an important element in its national health plan. Exhaustive studies of this regular practice of engaging deeply with the woods have demonstrated extraordinary health benefits, including lower blood pressure, lower stress levels, and even lower glucose levels.[10] Several books on forest bathing have been written, and the Association of Nature and Forest Therapy Guides and Programs has trained hundreds of guides to engage people with the forest more intimately. Says founder Amos Clifford: "The forest is the therapist; the guide opens the door."[11]

In writing about forest bathing in her beautiful and provocative book, *Earth & Soul*, Leah cautions us that while we are with the trees, we not just focus "only on the benefits to ourselves. Such self-absorption would not serve a friendship, a marriage, or a soul connection." Instead, we might consider "becoming curious about their connections, tuning in to their needs, and offering appreciation for their gifts to the world."[12]

While the forest can offer momentary calm and comfort, we are invited into a much deeper, more intimate, more reciprocal, and in many ways, more challenging relationship with the trees. I read somewhere that the sign of spiritual maturity is the ability to hold two seemingly conflicting truths concurrently. If we can walk in the forest with eyes and heart wide open, we see both growth and decay, beauty and despair, gifts to receive and gifts to give, life and death.

Like Thurman, Anne Frank, Becky, and the bereaved father, we, too, can take out our own pain and suffering and release it to the communion of the forest. We can meet the trees in mutual woundedness and with them share our most tender, vulnerable places. In turn, the trees reach out to us to offer companionship, comfort, and healing.

Adaptation and Resilience

The myriad interlocking personal and communal challenges we face today, especially the impacts of climate change, will require us to develop a new and different kind of resilience. These times will require a resilience that is adaptive, persistent, collaborative, and accepting. Trees offer us invaluable lessons on how we can find the tools we need not just to survive but also to thrive as we confront a complex array of environmental, political, cultural, and social issues.

Trees are constantly being challenged by weather, insects, predatory animals, fire, and human intervention. It is a way of life for them, and they are gifted at meeting these challenges with fascinating adaptations. We have all observed trees that are so full of twists and turns that they could inspire a Dr. Seuss book. These trees will do almost anything to reach the sun's light. Sometimes, unfettered by obstacles, they grow straight up to the sun. However, as it is in our human lives, there are many times when light simply isn't available. Something, or someone, casts a shadow and blocks the needed light. In those times, trees grow differently to get the nurture they need—sideways, at an angle, whatever it might take. Smaller understory trees, like dogwoods and redbuds, have even adapted to leaf out early in the spring to get ahead of larger neighbor trees.

And other times, trees can't grow much at all, so they don't. They wait it out, until conditions improve so that they once again can reach for the light. Some display trunks or branches that have been split by the elements or cut by humans. It seems a devastating loss, but oftentimes they continue to sprout new growth. Branches twist and curve, dodging other trees, reaching around obstacles, searching for the light. Roots push up walkways and foundations, extend over large distances above ground to find soil or connect to kin. Hard places like city streets or fields of stone, where concrete and asphalt dominate, would seem to block the spirit of trees; yet trees often stand in the smallest of spaces with the minimum of soil, still glorious even in their limitations. Wounds, burls, splits, and lost limbs may have slowed the growth of so many trees, yet they persevere. Our steady gaze bears witness to the loss and still celebrates these twisting, turning, beautiful resilient trees.

During times of water shortage, deciduous trees will start dropping their leaves from the top down, since they require the most energy to pull water from the roots.[13] As we mentioned in chapter 5, some desert trees will stop growing completely if water is inadequate. Conversely, trees like silver maples and sycamores, who live on riverbanks, have adapted hearty root systems that will withstand regular flooding. Naturalists often say that these trees "don't mind getting their feet wet."

Trees have also adapted to be very resilient, even aggressive, in their own defense. The force that animates all life surges within them, and they will do everything possible to keep themselves alive. At the first sign of an intrusion, tree cells "mount a robust defense" with "their arsenal of evasive chemistry."[14] And, as we discussed earlier, in given years, oak trees starve out predators by limiting acorn production. Then, within the next year or two, they will produce thousands of acorns so that the depleted squirrel and rodent population leave plenty of acorns to become new oak saplings.

Often when we walk in the forest, we notice large bumpy wooden protrusions called *burls* on the sides of trees. Burls usually result from an insect or microbial intrusion. If the intrusions are not deadly, the tree simply grows around the wound. Just like our large tulip tree, she lives on but differently. She adapted to the circumstances she faced, using whatever resources were still available to her to survive. Like the tulip tree that comforted the bereaved father, trees model for us how to adapt to seemingly devastating injuries and wounds.

We have observed too often lately how out-of-control wildfires can be deadly and destructive. But, in a more natural environment, many tree species have evolved not only to withstand fire but also to become completely dependent on it. The ponderosa and longleaf pines need fire to open their tough cones and release their seeds. The only way these pines can reproduce is in the presence of intense heat. The heat is life giving. As it is for our tree kin, sometimes the extreme heat of challenging circumstances can penetrate our own rough exteriors and release the seeds of new ways of seeing and participating in bringing health and wholeness to ourselves as well as all members of our Earth family.

A New Way of Being

I recently participated in a retreat, at a sprawling camp in central Maine, for national faith-based climate activists. The participants are on the front lines of climate action. We came to Maine exhausted, discouraged, bereft. Throughout our few days together, we opened ourselves to the wisdom of the lovely oak-maple-hemlock forest in which we were meeting.

The attendees participated in a number of spiritual exercises in which we took out our enormous grief for the planet and mourned with the forest. We found woundedness within the trees. We wrote lament poems. We grieved with them. We wept with them.

Alongside the death and decay in the forest, we also found new growth and healing. We observed the fir trees as they adapted to darkness by twisting and turning toward the light. We admired the maples as their roots curled to hold fast to the bank of the lake. And throughout, we delighted in the majesty of the hemlock, the tiny orange fungi that dotted dead logs, the multicolored butterflies, and using ultraviolet flashlights, the discovery of previously unseen flower parts. Bearing witness to the grief of the world cracked us open not only to sorrow but also to beauty, wonder, and awe. In turn, wonder and awe increased our capacity to hold grief.

The beautiful but ragged second-growth forest surrounding us became an active participant in our wanderings. We discussed the fact that a few hundred years before, another forest would have been found in this place. Huge pines, hundreds of years old, would have towered over the landscape. Wildflowers, wild blueberries, and ferns would have found footing in the gaps in the forest canopy. Bears, foxes, and moose would have roamed the woodlands. Wabanaki peoples could have been seen hunting deer and fishing in local streams, as well as weaving their beautiful baskets.

That rich, diverse old-growth forest no longer exists due to aggressive timber harvesting, first for shipbuilding and then for lumber and paper. The second-growth forest that replaced it cannot be the same forest. This loss deserves lament and grief. Yet participants often remarked that the newer forest's stately spruces and lush undergrowth was still stirring, calming, and healing. We noticed woodpeckers and warblers, foxes, and deer as well as many frogs, snakes, and insects. While the second-growth forest cannot be the same as the glorious old-growth forest, it can still thrive and give shade, nurture, comfort, and protection to countless human and nonhuman organisms.

In a world that is changing so dramatically, these activists knew that we could not look back and expect our lives, our forests, and our planet to be the same as they used to be. We are living second-growth lives now. Yet we found hope in experiencing firsthand the gifts that were being offered by this new and very different forest, and we were reminded of the gifts that we could all offer to it as well.

As we boarded the bus at the end of the retreat, we all seemed a little lighter to me. We were chatty and laughing, sharing contact information and plans to meet up with each other. The enormity of our mission had not changed. Yet our loads had been lightened by the sharing of grief, story, and slivers of hope with the woods and each other.

We can draw some comfort in the fact that, like us, trees are not alone in responding to threats, instead relying on a wide range of creatures and organisms to aid in their defense. At the first sign of danger to one tree, she sends chemical warning signals to her neighbors, who respond by strengthening their own chemical defenses. Trees attract the very birds and bugs who eat the insects and microorganisms that would otherwise cause them harm. Even frogs get into the act by eating would-be predators.[15] We discussed these communal connections in more detail in chapter 7.

One of the participants in the Maine retreat, Joelle Novey, who leads a very active DC-area, faith-based environmental group, was particularly moved by her experience with fellow activists. She recounted in a recent sermon how touched she was by the practice of going out into the woods and finding an element of nature that was attracting her and then asking the question, "What is it like to be you?"

> I generally experience nature as just the wallpaper to my story and my activities—the very definition of our world "environment." . . . But this one question—What is it like to be you?—transformed the forest into a community of beings, each on our own journeys, doing our best to make our way, sometimes finding sustenance and sometimes encountering difficulty.

She went on to say that she stands in two places. She holds the hope she sees in the work of the many who are transforming their lives and communities to make them more sustainable. At the same time, she constantly asks herself: "How can we bear to live in this moment?" The answer she received from her time in the forest came to her in Hebrew: "*B'yachad.* Together. Mindful of our one-ness."[16]

Spiritual Resilience–Showing Up, Acceptance, and Surrender

Our current planetary and cultural crises shake the underpinnings of our most basic spiritual understandings. Is there a benevolent life-giving force at work in the world? Are we on our own, or is there a Unity that binds us all together? Is there movement toward wholeness and reconciliation, or are planetary systems based on a series of random events?

These questions bring us to a significant aspect of resilience—one that is also strengthened by time in the forest—*spiritual resilience*. Simply put, spiritual resilience is showing up—fully and deeply with our whole being and whole heart.[17] It's being completely present to this moment, in all its complexities. It's being open to seeing and accepting the hard realities of these times as well as the opportunity for joy and renewal. It's reaching deep down within ourselves to realize our own potential for meeting challenges with courage and grace. In our spiritual resilience, we empty ourselves of control, wants, and expectations. In that emptiness, we meet the Deep Knowing that can give us the wisdom and clarity to meet this moment.

Though trees fight aggressively to survive and thrive, unlike humans, they don't spend a lot of time ruminating or struggling with the adaptations they must make to do so. Like most nonhuman creatures, they just accept, respond, and carry on. I am reminded of the three-legged dog who would happily run down the street near my childhood home, seemingly oblivious to his limitation. There is no struggle against adversity in nature, just response and surrender to the natural forces at play.

Unlike their human kin who often envy and strive to be different or better, trees simply are who they are and are satisfied to be so. They do not actively want for more. They do not yearn to be anything else. A red oak is not envious of a white oak because the white oak's bark is so beautifully plated. A dogwood does not complain that it will never be as tall as the hickory. And the sweet gum does not make long lists of what he should do to become more successful, fitter, or happier.

Trees seem to understand viscerally what spiritual teachers across the ages have tried to teach us. Surrender and acceptance are the heart of the spiritual life.

Much of human suffering, Buddhism holds, is caused by our grasping for, and clinging to, wants, desires, and expectations. Acceptance is at the center of the RAIN practice, which sets forth Buddhism's "four principles of the mindful transformation" that are available to us during challenging times. RAIN, widely taught by a variety of mindfulness teachers, includes first recognition of a specific challenge; then a sitting with it and letting it be accepted and absorbed deeply; followed by an investigation of how we experience it in our body, feelings, and mind; and finally a nonidentification with the challenge, which brings with it the end of clinging and the beginning of peace.[18] Without acceptance, Buddhists teach, moving through and out of difficult experiences is impossible.

Wisdom teacher Cynthia Bourgeault maintains that surrender is "at the root of everything. Without it, all the other spiritual practices remain merely pious busywork." Anyone who has ever met Bourgeault, a salty Mainer who lived for years on a remote island off the coast of Maine, would understand that she is not talking about meekly lying down in the face of adversity. Rather, surrender suggests an *awakening* to, and acceptance of, the *feelings* around what is, without controlling, forcing, or trying to make them anything other than what they are.[19] This cracked-open posture invites us to take in, deeply and completely, the joy, the despair, the challenge, and the delight of what is happening at this very moment, undistracted by what might have been or what might be. When we are able to engage in this *letting be*, she says that we are met with "an explosion of presence that goes off within us that is simultaneously an encounter with the wisdom master."[20]

Priest and prophet Thomas Merton, himself a wounded and complicated man, had a profound and close relationship with the forest, where he was able to experience most directly the presence Bourgeault describes. Throughout his life, he yearned to spend time in the quiet of the trees, where he could find the peace he so desperately sought. Finally, when he begged the abbot of his monastery for greater seclusion and time with the trees, the abbot assigned Merton the job as forester to restore the cutover monastic lands. Isolated in the damaged woods, he found the solitude, silence, and peace he needed to write some of his most important works: "The silence of the forest is my bride . . . and out of the heart of that dark warmth comes the secret that is heard only in silence, but it is the root of all the secrets that are whispered."[21]

Perhaps it is in our mutual woundedness that the forest offers its greatest gift—the gift of quiet and spaciousness where the Spirit, through her dark warmth, can touch us, calm us, heal us, and give us guidance and courage for our times. And in this silence, if we listen closely, we might be able to hear the holy whisper that reveals, unlocks, and opens us to the holy secret of all living things.

Bringing It Home: Spiritual Practice

Intention
To connect intimately with how your teacher tree has responded to her woundedness and challenges and learn lessons from her that will help you adapt to, accept, and heal your wounded places.

Description
As you walk slowly to your teacher tree, observe her from afar and then continually come closer. Notice ways she has had to twist and turn to reach light. Observe large burls

that have formed over her wounded places. See how she has sealed gashes in her trunk. Note the way her roots have adapted to a variety of different conditions. Notice any gaps in her canopy and how she has responded to them. Observe evidence of insects chewing on her leaves and how she has responded. In general, look for ways your teacher tree has met challenges with adaptation, acceptance, and resilience.

After observing your teacher tree for a while, write a six-word story that describes how she responds to the challenges she has faced. Using fewer words sometimes allows us to get to the heart of the matter.

If you are comfortable, you might ask her for any guidance she might offer to you in meeting the challenges you face or the grief with which you are living, be it personal, communal, ecological, societal, or otherwise.

CHAPTER 10

GRATITUDE AND RECIPROCITY

LEAH

Our first responsibility, the most potent offering we possess, is gratitude.

—ROBIN WALL KIMMERER,
"RETURNING THE GIFT"

Imagine a hot July in the middle of Kansas in the 1950s. Afternoon temperatures reached the midnineties, and shade trees were in short supply. Accessible by a dirt road, the four-room house where we lived sat in the middle of a field of ripening wheat and wells pumping crude oil from shale below. The wet towels Mom had hung at the open windows in hopes of tempering the hot winds moderated the indoor temperature only slightly. During the mornings, I entertained myself by playing with our cocker spaniel, feeding the chickens, trying to catch a stray cat, and casting flitting meadowlarks as the heroes in the stories I told to myself as I sat twisting on the swing that Dad built.

By midafternoon, the air hung heavy, sweat trickled down the back of my neck, and my cropped bangs stuck to my forehead. The only remedy was to seek refuge by lying under the cottonwood tree. Her triangular toothed leaves dangled in the gentle breeze, shimmered in the light, and occasionally clattered to a wind-beat that only she could hear. I sang softly to myself as I rested within the patterns of mottled shade.

Later, as I rode in the back of the family Chevy, my nose pressed against the window, I saw other cottonwoods and noticed how they stayed close to dry stream banks. I dreamed of living in a home under these magnificently spreading beauties, their bright green canopies offering protection from a relentless sun in an endless, cloudless sky.

Ways of cooling the places where we live and work are becoming even more important in our rapidly heating world. In urban areas where roads and buildings absorb and then radiate the heat of the sun, *heat islands* amplify the already intensifying temperatures by one to seven degrees Fahrenheit.[1] It's little surprise that the health and well-being of people, plants, and animals are compromised in such situations.

The picture shifts, however, where there are urban forests, green spaces, and generous shade trees. Through their gifts of shade and evapotranspiration, trees lower temperatures. Lower temperatures not only feel better, but they also decrease ground-level ozone that spikes on hot days in urban areas.[2] An Environmental Protection Agency website entitled "Using Trees and Vegetation to Reduce Heat Islands"[3] speaks to the special importance of trees in our cities.

Yet there's something fundamentally misleading when we write about "using trees," as if the trees were being programmed by humans to serve our needs. Language indicating that nature is at our disposal to *use* as we see fit is deeply embedded in our culture. Our focus is slanted toward *taking* what we want from nature rather than on *receiving* what she offers. Terms like *natural resources* and *ecosystem services* deny our relationship with other living beings and invite us to interact in ways inappropriate to kin we care about and who care for us. Deep connections to trees that are so important to body, heart, and soul are frayed when seen through the lens of *consumer* and *product*.

Yet despite this cultural tendency to distance ourselves from trees and their lives, it often takes us only a moment to recall a time when we felt a strong sense of connection to them. There is a deep knowing within us that we are recipients of many wonderous, beautiful, life-enriching, and sustaining gifts from trees. When we pause to touch into these memories, we can sense the well of gratitude within us. Minimal prompting stirs memories for me of sitting under a deep-rooted cottonwood, her leaves alight with the music of the breeze, cooling shade and delicate green dancing against cloudless blue.

Gratitude invites us into a world of gifts where we may *receive* what is offered instead of *taking* what we want when we want it. In this space, the demands of our ego take a backseat to our compassionate heart. Shifting our perspective from *thoughtlessly using* to *gratefully receiving* from the trees is a gift that keeps on giving. Feeling thankful has been shown to improve our sleep, mood, and immunity. Practicing gratitude can decrease anxiety, depression, and chronic pain. Keeping a gratitude journal allows us to notice and remember the gifts we receive daily.[4]

Gratitude is a feeling, an attitude, a language, and a bridge to deeper relationships and a powerful spiritual practice. From a place of gratitude, we remain more open, available, and connected to life as it unfolds. With an open heart of gratitude, we can acknowledge loss and grief—even allow our hearts to break—as we also behold the beauty, awe, and wonder of the world around us. As we sense more fully the gifts of trees, we see greater abundance and less scarcity, notice the potential for collaboration instead of competition, and sense how oneness exposes the myth of separation. This is spiritual wisdom to light our way.

Living in a Cycle of Giving and Receiving

Trees live within a cycle of giving and receiving. Sometimes they thrive only because of the gifts they exchange with others. Previously, we noted how birch and fir trees give nutrients to each other when most needed. We remarked how old-growth beech trees share resources with their younger kin. Tiny acorns from oak trees provide food to birds and squirrels. Sometimes nuts fall to the forest floor from full beaks or are buried and abandoned by forgetful squirrels, thus enabling the propagation of oaks trees beyond the spread of the mother tree. Woodpeckers and other birds pick out insects and pathogens harmful to the trees as they receive the gifts of food and places to nest. Giving and receiving. Reciprocity.

Northern flying squirrels feed on truffles that thrive at the base of red spruce trees. As they parachute through the forests of West Virginia, the squirrels disperse the spores and propagate truffles in the process. This is important because truffles are needed for a healthy spruce forest. These fungi grow intertwined with the roots of the red spruce, allowing the two organisms to exchange nutrients.[5] In response to this three-way reciprocity, spruce trees do not bow in gratitude, nor do the squirrel and truffle say a verbal thank you. Yet we see the fluid process of giving and receiving that sustains life. The web of reciprocity is continuously rewoven by relationships that support mutual thriving.

We recall that trees offer gifts to the human species as well. We eat the food of the forest, are sheltered by homes made from trees, and incorporate wood into our day-to-day lives from furniture to firewood, writing paper to books. Trees contribute to our every breath as they store carbon dioxide and emit oxygen. We have noted previously how trees refresh the air by filtering out pollutants and dangerous particulate matter through their leaves and needles. Leaves slow the impact of heavy rains. Expansive root systems in the underground network help to stabilize the land, act as sponges to slow potentially damaging stormwater runoff, and filter water before it reaches underground rivers.

Trees are critical to the stability and health of all of Earth. They store carbon, regulate climate, mediate the water cycle, support soil health, and sustain ecosystems and biodiversity. As author and educator David George Haskell wrote in *The Forest Unseen: A Year's Watch in Nature*, "Trees are masters of integration, connecting and unselfing their cells into the soil, the sky, and thousands of other species."[6] It's almost impossible to overstate the degree to which we humans, all living beings, and our Earth systems, depend on the gifts of trees and forests.

We live within an ongoing cycle of gifts. As we pause to reflect on the scope and multiplicity of blessings that trees provide day in and day out, we may find it nearly impossible to imagine how we can express the fullness of our gratitude and reciprocate fully. Here again, we can look to the trees for wisdom; always their lives are entwined in relationships of giving and receiving, a practice of reciprocity.

Exploring Reciprocity

Longing to become a full participant in a cycle of gifts and recognizing our responsibility to do so is a powerful opening to richer connections with trees and the ecosystems in which they participate. Yet I have grown to realize that I must listen for and learn the needs of trees before I am able to offer appropriate gifts in response to the abundance that I've received. There are too many examples of ways that my humancentric, results-oriented focus has not resulted in the positive outcome for which I'd hoped.

A dozen years ago, I chose a ginkgo for our yard because I loved its beautiful leaves. Shortly after planting that ginkgo, I learned that, unlike the native oak that feeds hundreds of caterpillars, ginkgoes support five or fewer such critters. The tree I found so attractive originated in China and held very little value for native birds or other wildlife of the eastern United States. By prioritizing my own desires without considering the needs of other beings, my efforts contributed little to mutual well-being. To give a gift that no one wants or needs is no gift at all.

I am not alone in acting first and learning later. For decades, many wooded areas were thinned heavily to allow light to reach smaller trees and stimulate their growth. We failed to note the wisdom of mother trees, who shade their young for years, allowing them to grow slowly and preserve their resources. Slow-growing trees may become longer-living trees for many species. Overly aggressive thinning trees can allow too much light to reach the forest floor, dry out the soil, and accelerate the growth of thorny shrubs, grasses, and berry bushes. This newly available food supply attracts deer and other wild game, who now have gained easy access to tasty snacks from the leaves and branches of small trees. To participate in the cycle of reciprocity requires an understanding of what truly constitutes a gift for others.

Discovering the best ways to contribute can be challenging and requires curiosity, deep listening, and perhaps even trial and error. In *Braiding Sweetgrass*, author Robin Wall Kimmerer shared the true story of Franz Dolp, an economist and writer turned volunteer forester. After moving to forty acres of what had been an old-growth forest of massive cedars in the Oregon Coast Range, Dolp was drawn to help the ravaged land, even if he was not always clear what steps were required.

He realized that to understand how to begin restoration, he would need to establish connections to the place. In the journal he kept, Dolp wrote: "It is important to engage in restoration with development of a personal relationship with the land and its living beings."[7] He began slashing by hand through the brush and brambles of blackberries and salmonberries, clearing a way for replanting native species. Over a period of eleven years, he and his partner, Dawn, planted thirteen thousand cedar, fir, and hemlock seedlings. "I was a temporary steward of this land. I was its caretaker," Dolp wrote. "More accurately I was its care-giver. . . . This was a forest of intimacy."[8]

Dolp dedicated himself to listening to, and learning alongside, the trees. It was not always a smooth process. He planted cedars on stream banks, only to discover that beavers loved to eat them. He tried fencing in the trees, but that did not work. Then he planted willows in hopes of distracting the beavers from the tasty cedars. The stream bank family would not bend to his desire. Acknowledging the need to keep learning from the forest community, he wrote, "I definitely should have met with a council of mice, boomers, bobcats, porcupines, beaver, and deer before I started this experiment."[9]

Perhaps that statement was written tongue in cheek. Yet his comment reminds us how difficult it is to let go of our desire to restore trees to places they once thrived and instead pause to listen for what is being invited *now* by land, tree, and ecosystem. It seems that we all need to learn this lesson time and again. To serve the woods, our gifts must meet their needs. Those connections—soil, other trees, and a wide array of living beings—were fragmented or destroyed when the woods were clear-cut. We cannot replant trees into the web of connections in which they once thrived, for those relationships no longer exist. We must be guided by humility and curiosity to understand the evolving needs of trees and the web of community in which they live. This will require listening that originates in open-hearted connections, not from a drive for results born of our hubris.

We may feel called to restore the woods, but questions persist: Restore to what? Who decides? No forest is static; life there has been changing, altering over lifetimes far beyond our own. It is important that these questions give us pause. How can we give back to the forests that have been decimated? Author Cal Flyn reported on the state of a dozen destroyed, abandoned, and isolated areas where humans have been forbidden to enter. In one example, she found that thousands of endangered species were flourishing in the lush forests of the Korean peninsula's demilitarized zone in large part because they had been left alone to evolve diverse ecosystems, free from human intervention.[10]

Indeed, when large forests already have begun the work of reestablishing themselves, direct intervention may not be the best course of action. In *The Power of Trees: How Ancient Forests Can Save Us if We Let Them*, author and forester Peter Wohlleben argued that we may reintroduce some local plants and animals to offer a small boost to a long-lost forest, but if we hope to encourage the amazing complexity of a vibrant ecosystem, in many cases it is better if we humans leave the forest alone to do the work it knows best.[11]

We do not come to the forest as a musical conductor with a fully written score. At our best, we will be improvising with a community that already has been improvising to maintain life since the first intervention, natural or human, occurred. When trees and ecosystems are engaged in the work of self-healing, they may need only gentle encouragement, protection from additional disturbance, or perhaps someone to tell their story. Indigenous and place-based peoples have long moved in synchronicity with their home woodlands within the ancient forests of Europe, the great rainforests of the Congo and the Amazon, and in other parts of the Americas. Their reciprocal practices included clearing dried vegetation, performing controlled burning, adding trees to nurture ecosystems, and planting forest gardens to feed people and wildlife. And because an understanding between people and land was deeply intertwined, practices could be improvised further as situations changed.

Of course, sometimes embracing reciprocity may require bold and decisive action as well. The Asháninka community living along the Amazon near the Brazil-Peru border is engaged in a struggle with logging companies to reclaim and protect its land, at one point even blocking a group of tractors with residents' bodies.[12] In the Congo rainforest, women have established conservation committees in their villages to patrol and protect the forest from illegal timber harvesting.[13] Protecting old-growth forests, mother trees, and local woodlands is critical to the future of the planet.

What about huge efforts to replant trees? Even if we are well intentioned, we should tread carefully. From 2010 to 2015, Earth was gaining 4.3 billion trees a year and losing 7.6 billion, a trend that has roughly continued.[14] John Reid and Thomas Lovejoy, authors of *Ever Green*, encouraged us to begin with saving the amazing, complex forests alive now. The most important step we can take follows in the footsteps of the Asháninka and Congolese communities: protect the forests we have. Reid and Lovejoy wrote that it is also important to protect places that have been lightly logged so that they have the chance to return to fully functioning ecosystems. The third step, they wrote, is to plant trees and then assume the role of caretaker and protector. "Even those who live in a city can go out and write the first few lines of an ecological epic that may take a million twists and turns involving insects, birds, mushrooms, and wind over multiple human lifetimes."[15]

For the benefit of ecosystems and Earth herself, planting large stands of trees requires attention to the long view and thinking like a forest. Industrial farming is not a model for growing healthy forests. If nonnative species, monocultures, tree harvesting, or reclaiming land from established prairies, woodlands, or swamps are part of the plan, for example, we are a long way from understanding the needs of trees, their ecosystems, and our living world. Before jumping on the bandwagon of massive tree plantings, it's important to learn about the life of trees and forests. Fully engaging in the cycle of reciprocity is not about speedy actions that might assuage our guilt or stroke our egos. It is not even about *producing results* that we have deemed most important. We are called to listen deeply to the trees and allow them to guide us.

There's another concept that we might consider as we respond in gratitude to trees: *refugia*. This term refers to small pockets of protection, safe spaces that allow lives to avoid devastation and thrive again after the worst has passed. *In situ refugia*, sometimes called *resilient sites*, occur naturally in place; nonetheless, we might consider asking the woods if there are ways we can assist in cocreating safe harbors for species to survive in this rapidly changing world. We can also discern whether we have a role in supporting *ex situ refugia*, places where species can relocate in response to the destruction of their current habitat.

Perhaps for many of us, reciprocity will involve doing the best we can to love and care for the trees around us: offering water to the newest saplings in times of drought;

removing invasive kudzu, Japanese honeysuckle, and other vines that can choke the life out of trees; planting natives to replace those lost; replacing our lawns with native plants and trees; and supporting the protectors of threatened forests. In our growing love and respect for trees, we are likely to be called to a soul-searching exploration of how we are using wood products in our daily lives and what changes we might make—not from a sense of guilt but from a deep sense of gratitude for all that trees gift to us and to life on Earth and a desire to participate fully in the web of reciprocity.

Taking Reciprocity Personally

For decades, I led pilgrimages to holy sites in different countries. Many pilgrims were able to make deep connections to the sacred by setting apart time in their daily lives for spacious listening in these holy places. Yet I felt a growing concern for the ecological footprint of such travel and a strong awareness that it's *all* holy ground. Beth and I therefore began to collaborate on pilgrimages close to home, a time when we invited individuals to travel with the heart of a pilgrim to their own backyard, local park, nearby garden, or a single tree.

With a little guidance and a few recommended practices, these backyard pilgrims found that they could open their senses to details they had never noticed before, even within familiar settings. With their eyes closed, the sounds of birds, insects, and blowing leaves told a special story of the trees and their interactions. The scent of pine and cedar nudged awake connections that were too often hidden. The bark and leaves of various trees took on new meaning under gently probing fingertips. Practicing a soft gaze, pilgrims were able to sustain attention on a small area until tiny details emerged as if by magic. So much beauty and diversity exist all around us, yet it is too often dismissed or discounted precisely because it is close to home. By walking or sitting in nearby places with gentle curiosity and open hearts, people have found themselves unexpectedly awestruck, frequently bursting forth with poetry, and nearly always grateful for the beauty of this world.

We led one of these backyard pilgrimages online during the period of extreme isolation early in the COVID-19 pandemic. It was impossible for people to travel far from their homes, and they were getting itchy and more than a little cranky. We offered some initial instruction online, then invited participants to go—quite literally—to their own backyards or a local park to engage in spiritual practices.

During one backyard practice—What's it like to be you?—Beth invited people to find a critter, tree, or other plant that attracted them and spend about twenty minutes with that individual, getting to know her. She suggested they ask questions of their new acquaintance: "Where do you live? What do you eat? Do you have a family? What are you afraid of? Am I doing anything that causes you harm?"

After the practice was complete, the pilgrims came back online to share their observations. Most of the group had commented when one woman haltingly asked to share her experience. She told of how much she loved gardening and how proud she was of the gardens she had carefully manicured in her yard. She even had gone through years of coursework and practice to become a *master gardener.*

The experience of intimacy with another critter, however, challenged her.

She told of lying peacefully on her stomach on the cool shady ground under a beautiful spreading maple tree when a black ant came into view. While lying eye to eye with the ant, she asked her the questions we suggested. She was curious about her. She delighted in her. And she wondered how her work in the garden and yard had affected her. For the first time, she reflected to the group, she understood that there were thousands of organisms with whom she shared the yard, each deserving of a safe and nurturing home: "I am so humbled. How dare I call myself *master*? I'm not the *master* of anything."

I, too, am cultivating a practice of opening my senses to what is close around me. As I attend more closely to the trees, I catch glimpses of their needs. Still, I can be too quick to jump to conclusions based on what *I think* will be best for them. It's not always easy to renew our connections to the more-than-human world, so far removed are we from the time when communities held ceremonies and rituals, told stories, and sang songs affirming that they *were* nature. For nearly my entire life, I have been supported in *thinking about* far more often than *listening with* the trees. Time and again, I must remind myself to be fully present.

On the land that my husband and I are committed to protect and assist, the soil is compacted clay. We do not want to add damage by tilling or digging. To support soil regeneration, we covered the ground with wet newspaper and cardboard to suppress the buried seeds of invasives and tempt earthworms to join the community. Then we added rich compost born of the scraps we had diligently tended over the preceding year, some straw that covered the bed over winter, coffee grounds from our morning ritual, and sometimes dried horse or chicken manure. We also listened for the land's call for trees.

Among the trees we've planted is a *Hamamelis virginiana*, or witch hazel, a small native late-blooming tree with extraordinary yellow flowers that attract many insects, while many more feed on the bark and leaves. The insects beckon birds—including cardinals, chickadees, crows, jays, finches, orioles, sparrows, and thrushes—who feed on the bugs as well as on the seeds. When days grow short and little else is flowering, the fragrance of witch hazel flowers sometimes attract owlet moths and late-season bees in need of food. It's a lovely cycle of giving and receiving just outside the window where we sit with our morning coffee. I am enamored by the witch hazel's changing beauty, and I appreciate that she has been used as a medicinal for many generations, the leaves and bark made into teas and ointments to ease inflammation and soothe sensitive skin. Witch hazel requires little in return except for water in dry times, added compost, and occasional gentle pruning. In our cycle of reciprocity, everyone seems content.

This past autumn was a mast year for the oak trees, who dropped an abundance of acorns in nearby woods. In such years, there are always more acorns than can be eaten and distributed by squirrels and birds. I selected five nuts to plant in my garden bed last October. Because they need cold temperatures to germinate, I am hoping that overwintering in this rich soil will give the acorns a good start for a year or two before they can be planted into the conservation areas around our neighborhood—if they are willing.

The world is waiting for our gifts, eager for us to participate more fully in the cycle of reciprocity and mutual thriving. Some of us will be called to attend to the wider world. For others, we may begin our participation in the web of reciprocity in our own backyard. I am happy to have aligned with a group of neighbors in work we call Lawns to Life![16] This educational campaign reflects our intention to replace short-rooted, nonnative turf grass in our yards with native plants, shrubs, and trees to support native birds and insects, sequester carbon, reduce stormwater runoff, and minimize watering. We love sharing what we've learned with others who want to respond similarly. We have been encouraged by Professor Douglas Tallamy, University of Delaware, who wrote that if each American landowner were to convert just half their lawn to native plants, we could collectively restore "some semblance of ecosystem function to more than twenty million acres of what is now ecological wastelands." This Homegrown National Park would become the country's largest park system, larger than all national parks in the lower forty-eight states.[17]

To me, this project holds exciting potential. Yet I sense that it's important to change the conversation from *restoring ecosystem function* to *restoring the cycle of reciprocity*. This is wisdom that Indigenous peoples around the world have understood and tried to teach us for centuries. This is wisdom we know in our bones: it is a gift to respond in deep gratitude for the abundance that trees offer to us, all living beings, and the entire Earth. It is this spiritual practice that can help us to reweave connections with the living world, restoring our heart and soul in the process. This is what Franz Dolp discovered on those forty acres in

Oregon: "I may heal the land. Yet I have little doubt of the direction that the real benefits flow. An element of reciprocity is the rule here. What I give, I receive in return. . . . In restoring the land, I restore myself."[18]

In the ultimate dance of reciprocity, there is no beginning or end to the flow of gifts, no distinction between giver and receiver. Gratitude and reciprocity open us to a world of abundance and connection, invite us into rich and enlivening communion, and inspire us to embrace a spiritual practice modeled by the trees that ultimately enhances the well-being of all.

Bringing It Home: Spiritual Practice

Intention

To honor, acknowledge, be grateful for, and give back to the tree who has been sharing with you.

Description

Return to the tree you've been visiting regularly. Reflect on the gifts you have received from this tree. Sit in silence, allowing your mind to wander back over your time with her. Let images arise of what has been given to you.

When this seems complete, name aloud or silently the gifts you have received. Continue to open yourself to gratitude.

Return to silence, bringing your attention back to your teacher tree. Ask her what you might offer to her in gratitude for her generosity to you.

Take all the time you need for this practice. Feel free to repeat it often.

CHAPTER 11

RENEWAL AND HOPE

BETH

I wish for you
grounded hope
and room for you and the incomprehensible
to walk together.

—LAURA MARTIN, "WHAT I WISH FOR YOU"

In the many years that Leah and I have been leading classes, programs, walks, and retreats related to spirituality in nature, we always end with a time of discussion with the participants. Invariably, this question is raised in some form or the other: Do you have hope?

That question always gives us pause. It is broad and complex and personal. When we are asked the "hope question," we wonder: What kind of reassurance is the questioner seeking? And what do they mean when they use the term? Is hope associated with a specific outcome, as in *hoping for* something? Is it a longing to go back to a time or place or rather to move forward to a different way of being? Is hope a wish or maybe a prayer? Is hope something we might feel or is it more active and participatory?

Perhaps the trees might offer some clues to the nature of hope and renewal for our times.

Death and Rebirth

When I was a young US Senate staffer, I had the privilege of visiting Yellowstone National Park as the 1988 wildfires swept through the park. By any account, the fires were devastating. We traveled by van through the smoky landscape, watching the helicopters dropping tanks of water, brave firefighters digging fire lines, and the bright yellow blaze roaring through the forest. I was stunned by the extent of the destruction. The fires eventually burned close to 800,000 acres in the park and 1.4 million acres in the Greater Yellowstone Ecosystem. Tens of millions of trees were burned.[1]

During our visit, we met with National Park Service staff, including the park superintendent and the chief ecologist. The park superintendent was overwhelmed by the pressures of the moment, so much so that I worried for his health. State and federal officials were exerting enormous pressure on him to stop the fires. Local communities on the park boundaries were terribly concerned that their towns and homes would be destroyed. Park lovers around the world wondered if the park could ever recover from such devastating losses of trees, brush, and wildlife.

The chief ecologist had a completely different take on the situation. When we spoke with him, his words tumbled out excitedly. He told us about how decades of fire suppression had allowed an unnatural amount of underbrush and litter to build up in the forest, which in turn provided fuel for the fires. He was concerned about local communities and the many creatures affected, but at the same time, he was hopeful that the fires would help restore balance to the ecosystem, bring new young groves of trees, and provide more food for wildlife. I was unconvinced, as was the park superintendent.

Nearly thirty-five years after the fires completely altered the Yellowstone ecosystem, I returned to the park and was stunned by what I saw. Healthy groves of lodgepole pine grew on areas that had been completely burned out. Because sunlight had been able to reach the ground, undergrowth was rich. The soil was enriched by the detritus left behind and resulted in many new plants, which subsequently provided food for wildlife. The forests were not and will never be the same as before the fires. However, by all accounts, they are healthy and are providing sustenance to the rich diversity of the Yellowstone Ecosystem in new and exciting ways, just as the ecologist predicted.

It would be naive to suggest that the environmental damage we have done to forests, and the planet more generally, will magically result in a new healthy world. The Yellowstone fires caused terrible damage to the ecosystem and the neighboring human communities, which are still recuperating. We cannot recreate former forests any more than we can return to a pre-Industrial world, before much of the extensive environmental damage to the planet was done. Such planetwide losses need to be acknowledged and grieved.

Perhaps the Yellowstone forests are teaching us that part of our journey of hope is to hold both loss and grief even as we joyfully celebrate new life. We see clearly the destruction, and at the same time we see new life emerging from it. We grieve but do not fall into despair. We rejoice without giving into simplistic optimism.

Eternal Life

As we walk in the forest, we might keep an eye out for a large tree that has died and fallen on the forest floor. A close look might reveal moss growing on the log, evidence of woodpeckers pecking at its bark for insects, termites and other bugs digging inside of it, or perhaps a sapling growing out of it.

Death is an absolute necessity in a healthy forest. These dead trees provide essential nutrients for hungry birds, insects, worms, and microorganisms. They nurture the soil with important organic material. In streams, they provide cover and shade for aquatic organisms. These so-called *nurse logs* remind us that everything in nature is recycled, repurposed, and renewed. Death in the forest is inevitable. However, it never has the final word.

For generations, the common forestry practice was to take all the dead trees out of the forest. The theory was that they should not be left simply to decay and be "wasted" while they still had some commercial value. On public lands today, leaving *standing dead* and *dead and down* trees in the forest is understood to be important to a healthy forest ecosystem, and this practice is now more common, particularly in mature forests.

As I consider death in the forest, I am reminded of a time during my theological education when I was trying to come to grips with the concept of *eternal life*. I grew more and more confused and agitated as I pored through the complicated eschatological ruminations on eternal life from the "great" theologians. In a moment I'm not entirely proud of, I became so upset that I threw one of the *great* books across the room.

Soon after the book-throwing incident, I was walking in the forest and encountered a large cottonwood who had died and fallen years earlier. Moss, lichen, and fungi spread across her decaying bark. I peeled a piece of bark away and saw some happy millipedes running about through its tiny wooden tunnels. A red-spotted newt crawled from beneath her remaining trunk.

I then imagined that eventually this cottonwood would decay completely and become part of the soil, whose elements would then eventually become part of a fern, a fungus, a frog, or a human being. I realized that this majestic tree will in fact have eternal life. She will be recycled and reprocessed, her molecules rearranged into other organisms and plants and creatures, and she will live on.

The theological concept of eternal life still confounds me, and I've given up trying to make sense of it. But this understanding that everything in nature, including us if we allow it to be so, will live on in the bodies of other creatures provides enormous comfort, and yes, hope to me. Regardless of what the future brings, I know that life in some form or another will continue.

Participating in Change

Forest ecologists have long studied patterns by which forests mature, called *forest succession*. There is a great deal of variability within a forest, and its maturation depends on species composition, environmental factors, and some degree of randomness. However, many scientists see that there is a common progression that most forests follow. The cycle begins with a major disturbance, such as a storm event, fire, land clearing, or timber harvesting. In this scenario, most of the trees have been disturbed or destroyed by this event. If the disturbed land is left alone, herbs and grasses will come in, followed by smaller *pioneer species* of trees. These brave pioneers play a significant role in nurturing the soil and reestablishing the beginnings of a new forest on the site. In our mid-Atlantic region of the United States, those species might be black locust, pine, and cedar. Eventually, heartier, taller trees emerge and dominate the site.[2]

Forest ecologists teach us that while there is a relatively predictable cycle in forest succession, at the heart of the process is change. As much as we might cling to the hope that all can remain the same, change in the forest is unavoidable and necessary. In their comprehensive book on *Forest Ecosystems*, the authors maintain that "movement and change characterize every living system. Individuals grow and die, and throughout the lifetime of a high organism its cells are renewed many times."[3] Change in the natural world is inevitable.

While trees don't fight change, we humans often find change difficult to absorb, let alone accept. Taking in the magnitude of the ecological changes before us is particularly difficult. Buddhist philosopher and ecological activist Joanna Macy and psychologist Chris Johnstone say that uncertainty around the health of Earth is "the pivotal psychological reality of our time."[4] They warn, too, that numbing ourselves to the reality of our changing times is not the answer. It simply deprives us of the energy we need to participate in a creative response.

A warming planet affects and shifts everything—ecology, economics, politics, culture, and social justice. Clearly, there has been, and will continue to be, major disturbances and tragic losses in our planetary ecosystems. For the forest and our planet, our futures rely on the pioneers who will move into the disturbance, restabilize the networks, and provide the sustenance that will allow the forest to eventually mature to meet its potential.

Although hope requires that we look clearly into the face of loss and grief, it is rooted in the understanding that we are bathed in the gifts of the living world. We live on a planet that is oriented toward life. Hope beckons us to look with clear eyes at the disruption around us, acknowledge that change will be our constant companion, and at the same time participate in renewal based on our gifts and our calling. Perhaps we, too, can become pioneer species in the little plot of ground where we might find ourselves. In her inspiring book, *Hope in the Dark*, Rebecca Solnit wrote that "hope locates itself in the premises that we don't know what will happen and that in the spaciousness of uncertainty there is room to act."[5]

In 1379, builders completed the New College at Oxford University. Its centerpiece was an enormous dining hall supported by huge long beams running the full length of the room. Legend has it that local foresters knew that the oak beams of the roof would eventually decay and need to be replaced and that it would take several hundred years for the oaks to grow to the size of the existing large beams. Aware of the challenge that future generations would face, they planted a forest of oaks to provide new beams when needed. Five hundred or so years later, administrators found that, indeed, the beams were infested and weakened by insects and would need to be replaced. The now-enormous oaks were standing nearby, available to provide new wood for the decayed beams.[6]

The forests and the future that we plant and nurture today will mature well after we are gone. We will almost certainly not see the results of our efforts. The story of the forest and of our ailing planet is not yet written. We can barely imagine what the future might hold. There is opportunity, though, to participate in hope in the here and now by planting those literal and metaphorical seedlings and trusting that they will bear fruit in a future beyond our knowing.

Renewal and Mystery

About twenty years ago, we bought about twelve acres of land in the Blue Ridge Mountains. (Let's leave aside for a moment the concept of "buying" and "owning" land.) The land is in the middle of a beautiful deciduous and pine forest, including the ailing but still living black oak from chapter 3. When we first arrived, there were also several trailers in various states of repair on the property. The previous owner (there's that word *own* again) had lived in a tidy 20' x 10' red trailer surrounded by a perfectly manicured, lush green lawn about an acre in size.

For the next few years, we got to work restoring the land to be more "natural"—or rather what we deemed its natural state to be. We removed all the trailers, shored up the vernal pond that provided important habitat for local frogs and salamanders, whacked away at invasive trees and plants, and seeded the area where the trailers were with a native meadow mix to bring back its natural functioning.

At some point, we ran out of steam. Work and family pressures kept us away from the land for long periods of time, and we just couldn't get around to doing something about that very unnatural one-acre lawn. We knew that the grass growing there was neither natural nor helpful to the local ecosystem, had little capacity to absorb water or filter pollutants, and provided little habitat for local species. However, we just didn't have the energy to remove the lawn and replace it, so we ignored it.

One day, after a long absence, we pulled up the gravel drive and realized that what had been a lawn was no longer such. At least fifty tiny two-feet-high trees—Virginia pine and cedar—had established themselves through *natural regeneration*. Various animals and the wind had most likely picked up seeds from the nearby conifers and dropped them on the grassy area. Rain had buried them into the soil, and voilá, a forest was forming. These prototypical pine and cedar *pioneer species*—typically the first trees to come into a disturbed area—had moved in and taken over with absolutely no assistance from us.

Over the next few years, we did nothing but watch with amazement as the trees grew taller and taller. We saw blue jays, chickadees, and the glorious cedar waxwings (aptly on the cedar trees) come and go, as well as a mother turkey and her five chicks, who by the looks of it, had established a lovely home in the pine straw. We knew, too, that hundreds of thousands of other creatures were operating under the ground, nurturing the trees, breaking up the ground so roots could expand, transporting water up and down the trees—all unseen and unbeknownst to us.

At some point, our human controlling natures took hold, and we contacted the state forester, who came up and gave us a prescription to thin aggressively to make the forest "healthier."

Obligingly, on a scorching-hot summer day, we went into the forest with handheld saws and took down a few of the smaller trees. We promised ourselves that when the weather was better, we would finish the job and thin every five years or so, as recommended. We didn't, and we haven't.

The little forest-that-could is now thriving all by herself, with little intervention from us, just ample sun and rain from Mother Nature. By my eye, the tallest of the Virginia pines are now twenty-five feet tall, and the forest is lush and healthy. Nature has taken care of the less healthy trees by letting them go. And we still see evidence of those turkeys as well as deer and numerous birds. I am reminded of author and forester Peter Wohlleben's view that the forest has its own intelligence upon which we need to learn to rely: "They [forests] are places where information about solutions to problems are stored in the genetic material of organisms and in their interplay with each other. As the forest evolves, this knowledge is constantly being tested and added to."[7]

When I survey the rest of the surrounding land, I see where our little forest might go in the future, far beyond my lifespan. I see pines and cedars yielding to moderate-sized maples, hickories, and black gums, which in turn yield to oaks and tulip trees. Of course, dramatically warming temperatures could alter the forest's future as southern species migrate north for cooler temperatures. At that point, yet another progression might emerge, following familiar steps with a far different makeup of the forest.

Before I wrote this final chapter, I wandered down to the forest grove to see if it had any final words for us. On my way, I saw that the scrappy black oak I mentioned in chapter 3 had yet to develop those new lime-colored miniature leaves of spring, and I began to wonder if this is the year she will finally fall. The vernal pond next to the grove is full of spring rains since the water didn't actually go down the sewer as my granddaughter Daphne had suggested it had. As I walked, I saw many cracked-open acorns embedded in the soil, just waiting for new life to form within. I passed a fallen chestnut oak crawling with termites, ants, and beetles. Bluejays were squawking, and titmice were calling their familiar Peter-Peter-Peter.

I was overcome with the abundance of life—from huckleberries to earthworms to thorny smilax to pine straw, conjoining and collaborating. I knew, too, that in this place Divine Mystery—called by so many names—was present here—enlivening, nurturing, and connecting all beings in this sacred grove.

As I looked more closely, I noticed tiny cedars and pines—less than three feet tall—emerging in the sunny spots. I pictured their roots digging into the soft soil to establish themselves. I found myself wondering what they might know about the underground miracles taking place right now beyond my ability to see.

As I see these tiny saplings, I consider that for so many years, my husband and I couldn't imagine that in the soil beneath this once-lawn, something magical was happening. Beyond our seeing, beyond our knowing, a forest was being reestablished. I keep wondering—what else is happening beyond our sight? What other tricks does nature have up her sleeve? I can't help but wonder what miracles might be brewing beyond my imagination as Mystery and nature collaborate.

While hope calls us to participate actively in the renewal of the forest, it also beckons us to stop, slow down, and pay attention to the miracles unfolding all around us without any effort from us. We live into hope by knowing and trusting that there are forces at play beyond our sight and beyond our knowledge that are moving Earth and all her creatures toward reconciliation and rebirth.

A few months ago, I received a call from eighty-four-year-old Sally Johnson, who told me that "the gremlins were gone from her computer," and she had been able to watch the first session of our six-week class on the Spiritual Wisdom of Trees. She said she was "sufficiently cracked open and ready for more." Mrs. Johnson told me how much she loves being among the trees, where she doesn't "walk along" but rather "gawks along." Having recently moved into a senior community at the encouragement of her children, she expressed how much she misses her "little house in the woods." She said, "I was never lonely there because the birds and the animals and the trees kept me company."

In the course of our conversation, she told me a story about her father, who like Mrs. Johnson, had moved into a retirement community in his later years. Her father had become quite ill, and he knew that he did not have much time left to live. Mrs. Johnson started receiving regular calls and complaints from the retirement home about her father "escaping" from the home. They kept finding him in the woods across the road, sitting on the ground and leaning against his favorite maple tree, "with his back to the nursing home," Mrs. Johnson was quick to add. At some point, the powers-that-be in the retirement home called

Mrs. Johnson and insisted that she do something about her father continually wandering, getting lost, and needing to be rescued. She responded, "For goodness sakes, he doesn't need to be rescued. He's not lost. He knows where he is. Let him be."

Among the trees, we know where we are, and we know who we are. Like Sally Johnson and the scruffy little acorn in chapter 2, we are sufficiently cracked open and ready for more. We dig deeply into the Ground of our Being for insight and sustenance. We feel the life-giving water that circulates through the trees and all beings, including us. We eagerly look for the delight that is all around us just waiting to be discovered. We bathe in the warmth of the sun as well as learn hard lessons from the darkness. We adapt to, and bravely accept, our new reality and practice the resilience that has been so beautifully modeled for us by the trees. We grieve and we mourn, openly and actively. We do our part to live simply and reciprocally with our beloved trees. We find others—human and nonhuman—in our community of multitudes to be loving companions with us on this challenging, joy-filled journey. We live in the confidence that death does not and will not have the final word. We trust that there is something circulating within us and others in this complicated, interdependent, and interconnected world that will continue to enliven and renew. Through it all, we remain grateful.

And always, we attend to the wisdom of trees.

Bringing It Home: Spiritual Practice

Intention

To experience renewal and hope with your teacher tree and in the forest.

Description

Center yourself with a few cleansing breaths before you leave to go visit your teacher tree. On your way there, take a hope walk. Watch for buds forming, blossoming, bearing fruit, or just holding on during the winter. Notice the ways the forest has responded to storms or other major events by renewing itself. Observe new trees and other plants coming up from the ground. Watch for baby birds, foxes, deer, and the like.

See if you notice a dead tree lying on the forest floor. Spend some time with this tree and notice anything living on it—fungus, moss, lichen, perhaps a sapling. Gently take off a piece of bark and watch for a while. Observe any small insects, worms, termites, or other small creatures who are eating inside the dead tree. Notice how much life is being supported by this dead tree, this *nurse log*.

When you reach your teacher tree, spend some time with her. In a way that's comfortable for you, express gratitude to her for the time you have spent together and the wisdom she has shared with you. You can always take a hope walk, engage in any of the practices in this book, or visit your teacher tree whenever you like. The wisdom of trees is always available to you.

GRATITUDE

This section might have been the most difficult part of the book for us to write, as there are so many beings— human and nonhuman, living and no longer living—who have inspired us, guided us, and supported us, it would be impossible for us to acknowledge them all. We hope you know who you are.

Great thanks go to Adrienne Ingrum, our first editor, who believed in this book from the very beginning and offered very helpful feedback and encouragement throughout the writing process. We are also grateful for Lisa Kloskin, Adrienne Samuels, and the team at Broadleaf Books for helping bring *Discovering the Spiritual Wisdom of Trees* to fruition.

We appreciate the consistent support of the Center for Spirituality in Nature staff, board, and donors, who have made significant contributions to sustaining the center and us during the writing process. Special thanks to Payton Hoegh and Meighan Fraga for beautifully running the show as Beth absented herself for many months to attend to this book.

We are grateful, too, to the many program and retreat participants who have journeyed in the trees with us and have so informed and enhanced our own understanding of the spirituality so present in the forest.

And we each extend enormous gratitude to one another, as colleagues, collaborators, conversation partners, and friends. We were warned that writing a book together could be challenging both to the manuscript and to the friendship. We are so appreciative that working together on this book was very smooth, respectful, inspiring, relationship-enhancing, and so much fun. We know that our individual contributions to this endeavor are so much richer for our partnership.

And we know that writing a book is better with a village.

Beth

My village includes many dear friends and a growing family: my children, Charlie, Erin, and James; their spouses, Jen and Lyzz; and my siblings, Doug and Susan—who have cheered me on, encouraged me, and believed in me always. I am especially appreciative of my granddaughters, Lucy, Daphne, Charlie, Maggie, and Roe, who inspire me daily to be as curious and courageous as they are. Special thanks go to Rebecca and Joy, who have steadfastly supported me, this book, and the greater work of deepening our spirits in nature in too many ways to mention.

And, always, I send love and gratitude to my husband, Clint, who throughout the writing process listened, encouraged, read, and oh-so-diplomatically made suggestions, while at the same time attending to the many shared responsibilities I was ignoring.

Leah

I am grateful to live in a community with people who care about trees, plants, soil, and soul, and who offer endless encouragement to this sometimes-harried writer who takes on too many additional projects. I am so blessed to have a loving and supportive family. Andrew and Ana, thank you for encouraging and inspiring the work I do. I love you. Deep gratitude and love to David for reading my work through various stages of development, cheering me on, and keeping things running smoothly so that I could spend longer at my desk. This is what love looks like after all these years together. Thank you.

***

Finally, and most importantly, the authors offer immense gratitude to all the teacher trees, woods, and forests who have enriched our lives with wisdom and beauty—and who make all our lives possible.

NOTES

Chapter 1: Discovering Our Roots

1 Carolyn Finney, *Black Faces, White Spaces: Reimaging the Relationship of African Americans to the Great Outdoors* (Chapel Hill: University of North Carolina Press, 2014), 60.

Chapter 2: Cracking Open

1 Pema Chödrön, *When Things Fall Apart: Heart Advice for Difficult Times* (Boulder: Shambhala Publications, 2016), xiii.

2 Cynthia Bourgeault, *The Wisdom Way of Knowing: Reclaiming an Ancient Tradition to Awaken the Heart* (San Francisco: Jossey-Bass, 2003), 64–66.

3 Thomas Merton, "Hagia Sophia," *Ramparts Magazine*, March 1963, https://www.unz.com/print/Ramparts-1963mar-00065.

4 William McNamara, quoted in Walter J. Burghardt, "Contemplation: A Long, Loving Look at the Real," *Church* (Winter 1989), 14–17.

5 Cynthia Bourgeault, *The Wisdom Jesus: Transforming Heart and Mind—a New Perspective on Christ and His Message* (Boulder: Shambhala Publications, 2008), 35–36.

6 Alice Brice, "After Thoughts: Dacher Keltner on the Science of Awe and Psychedelics," *Berkeley News*, February 22, 2021, https://news.berkeley.edu/2021/02/22/after-thoughts-dacher-keltner-on-awe-and-psychedelics.

7   John O' Donohue, *Beauty: The Invisible Embrace* (New York: Harper Collins, 2003), 12.
8   Fred Hageneder, *The Meaning of Trees: Botany, History, Healing, Lore* (San Francisco: Chronicle Books, 2005), 8.
9   Hageneder, 8.
10 Belden C. Lane, *The Great Conversation: Nature and the Care of the Soul* (New York: Oxford University Press, 2019), 89.
11 Douglas Wood, *Fawn Island* (Minneapolis: University of Minnesota Press, 2001), 4.
12 "Omeka@CTL | UVM Tree Profiles: Eastern Red Cedar: Native Cultural Significance," accessed October 8, 2023, https://libraryexhibits.uvm.edu/omeka/exhibits/show/uvmtrees/eastern-red-cedar/eastern-red-cedar-native-signi.
13 Bill Plotkin, "Inscendence: The Key to the Great Work of Our Time (A Soulcentric View of Thomas Berry's Work)," in *Dreamer of the Earth: The Spiritual Ecology of the Father of Environmentalism,* ed. Ervin Laszlo and Allan Combs (Rochester, VT: Inner Traditions, 2011), 42–71.
14 Maria Popova, "Anam Cara and the Essence of True Friendship: Poet and Philosopher John O'Donohue on the Beautiful Ancient Celtic Notion of Soul-Friend," *The Marginalian* (blog), August 12, 2015, https://www.themarginalian.org/2015/08/12/anam-cara-john-o-donohue-soul-friend/.

Chapter 3: The Wonder of Trees

1   Belden C. Lane, *The Great Conversation: Nature and the Care of the Soul* (New York: Oxford University Press, 2019), 5.
2   Bernd Heinrich, *The Trees in My Forest* (New York: Cliff Street Books, 1997), viii, ix.
3   David Burnie, *Tree: Discover the World of Trees—from Tiny Saplings to Forest Giants* (London: DK Publishing, 2005), 6–7.
4   Tristan Gooley, *How to Read a Tree: Clues and Patterns from Bark to Leaves* (New York: The Experiment, 2023), 298.
5   Robin Wall Kimmerer, *Braiding Sweetgrass: Indigenous Wisdom, Scientific Knowledge, and the Teachings of Plants* (Minneapolis: Milkweed Editions, 2013), 221, 222.
6   Tom Wessels, *Forest Forensics: A Field Guide to Reading the Forested Landscape* (Woodstock, VT: Countryman Press, 2010), 7.
7   Wessels, *Forest Forensics,* 7.

8   Katherine J. Wu, "Alternatives to Heterosexual Pairings, Brought to You by Non-Human Animals," *Smithsonian Magazine*, June 28, 2018, https://www.smithsonianmag.com/science-nature/alternatives-heterosexual-pairings-brought-you-non-human-animals-180969481/.

9   The Cary Institute, "Oak Facts," November 3, 2023, https://www.caryinstitute.org/sites/default/files/public/downloads/curriculum-project/the_oak_tree_facts.pdf.

10 Burnie, *Tree*, 14.

11 Joanna Mounce Stancil, "The Power of One Tree: The Air We Breathe," US Department of Agriculture, March 17, 2015, https://www.usda.gov/media/blog/2015/03/17/power-one-tree-very-air-we-breathe.

12 Hermann Hesse, *Wandering*, trans. James Wright (New York: Farrar, Straus & Giroux, 1972), 57.

13 Margaret Lowman, "CanopyMeg," accessed October 19, 2023, https://canopymeg.com/.

14 J. M. Sillick and W. R. Jacobs, "Healthy Roots and Healthy Trees—2.926," Colorado State Extension, accessed November 3, 2023, https://extension.colostate.edu/topic-areas/yard-garden/healthy-roots-and-healthy-trees-2-926/.

15 Peter Wohlleben, *The Hidden Life of Trees: What They Feel, How They Communicate* (Vancouver: Greystone Books, 2016), 82–83.

16 Richard Grant, "Do Trees Talk to Each Other?" *Smithsonian Magazine*, March 2018, https://www.smithsonianmag.com/science-nature/the-whispering-trees-180968084/.

17 Andrew Kling, "The Mystery of Marcescence," University of Maryland Extension, March 1, 2022, https://extension.umd.edu/resource/mystery-marcescence.

18 Douglas W. Tallamy, *The Nature of Oaks: The Rich Ecology of Our Most Essential Native Trees* (Portland, OR: Timber Press, 2021), 76.

19 Suzanne Simard, *Finding the Mother Tree: Discovering the Wisdom of the Forest* (New York: Knopf, 2021), 287.

Chapter 4: Soil

1   Nyle C. Brady and Ray R. Weil, *The Nature and Properties of Soils* (Uttar Pradesh, India: Pearson, 2014), 30.

2   David A. Perry, Ram Oren, and Stephen C. Hart, *Forest Eco-systems* (Baltimore: Johns Hopkins University Press, 2008), 256.

3   Brady and Weil, *The Nature and Properties of Soils*, 202.

4   Soil Association, accessed March 26, 2024, https://www.soilassociation.org/causes-campaigns/save-our-soil/.

5   Perry, Oren, and Hart, *Forest Ecosystems*, 300.

6   Seon-Ok Kim et al., "Psychophysiological and Metabolomics Responses of Adults during Horticultural Activities Using Soil Inoculated with Streptomyces Rimosus: A Pilot Study," *International Journal of Environmental Research and Public Health* 19, no. 2 (2022): 12901, https://www.mdpi.com/1660-4601/19/19/12901.

7   James Weldon Johnson, *God's Trombones: Seven Negro Sermons in Verse* (New York: Penguin Books), 17.

8   Paul Tillich, *Systematic Theology*, vol. 1 (Chicago: University of Chicago Press, 1951), 235–36.

9   Publications Office of the European Union, "Soil: The Hidden Part of the Climate Cycle," 2011, https://climate.ec.europa.eu/system/files/2016-11/soil_and_climate_en.pdf.

10 Todd A. Onti and Lisa A Schulte, "Soil Carbon Storage," *Nature Education Knowledge* 3, no. 10 (2012): 35, https://www.nature.com/scitable/knowledge/library/soil-carbon-storage-84223790/#:~:text=Since%20the%20industrial%20revolution%2C%20the,the%20atmosphere%20(Lal%20 2009).

11 Brady and Weil, *The Nature and Properties of Soils*, 35.

12 Gayle Boss, *All Creation Waits: The Advent Mystery of New Beginnings* (Brewster, MA: Paraclete Press, 2016), 54–56.

Chapter 5: Water

1   "Learning Activities—Water," Indigeneous Steam, accessed March 28, 2024, https://indigenoussteam.org/learning-activities/water/#:~:text=Indigenous%20peoples%20have%20deep%20relationships,more%2Dthan%2Dhuman%20relatives.

2   Richard Connor and Michela Miletto, "The United Nations World Water Development Report 2023: Partnerships and

Cooperation for Water," UNESCO, 2023: 2, https://unesdoc.
unesco.org/ark:/48223/pf0000384657.

3 Lindsey Purcell, "How Do Trees Use Water?" *Purdue University Landscape Report* 21, no. 14 (August 24, 2021), https://www.
purduelandscapereport.org/article/how-do-trees-use-water/.

4 Ben Shouse, "Trees Smuggle Water to Fungi," *Science* (October 24, 2022), https://www.science.org/content/article/trees-smuggle-water-fungi.

5 Peter Wohlleben, *The Hidden Life of Trees: What They Feel, How They Communicate* (Vancouver: Greystone Books, 2016), 48.

6 Wohlleben, *The Hidden Life of Trees*, 56.

7 US Forest Service, "Water and Forests: The Role Trees Play in Water Quality," *Forests* 1, no. 2 (1999), https://www.fs.usda.
gov/Internet/FSE_DOCUMENTS/stelprdb5269813.pdf.

8 David George Haskell, *The Forest Unseen: A Year's Watch in Nature* (New York: Viking, 2012), 74.

9 Wohlleben, *The Hidden Life of Trees*, 56–58.

10 Anne Post, "Why Fish Need Trees and Trees Need Fish," *Alaska Fish and Wildlife News* (November 2008), https://
www.adfg.alaska.gov/index.cfm?adfg=wildlifenews.
view_article&articles_id=407.

11 Post, "Why Fish Need Trees."

12 David A. Perry, Ram Oren, and Stephen C. Hart, *Forest Ecosystems* (Baltimore: Johns Hopkins University Press, 2008), 256.

13 Perry, Oren, and Hart, *Forest Ecosystems*, 34.

14 David Ellison et al., "Trees, Forests and Water: Cool Insights for a Hot World," *Global Environmental Change* 43 (March 2017), https://www.sciencedirect.com/science/article/
pii/S0959378017300134.

15 Ben Rawlence, *The Treeline: The Last Forest and the Future of Life on Earth* (New York: St. Martin's Press, 2022), 158.

16 Robin Wall Kimmerer, *Braiding Sweetgrass: Indigenous Wisdom, Scientific Knowledge, and the Teachings of Plants* (Minneapolis: Milkweed Editions, 2013), 55–56. Italics in the original.

17 Bron Taylor, *Dark Green Religion: Nature Spirituality and the Planetary Future* (Oakland: University of California Press, 2010), 150.

Chapter 6: Embracing Light and Dark

1   Peter Wohlleben, *The Hidden Life of Trees: What They Feel, How They Communicate* (Vancouver: Greystone Books, 2015), 162.

2   Steve Nix, "A Guide to the Tree 'Pioneers' That Create Forests," Treehugger, July 29, 2019, https://www.treehugger.com/pioneer-tree-species-1343080.

3   Tristan Gooley, *How to Read a Tree: Clues and Patterns from Bark to Leaves* (New York: The Experiment, 2023), 138.

4   Gooley, *How to Read a Tree*, 189.

5   Gooley, *How to Read a Tree*, 190.

6   Wohlleben, *The Hidden Life of Trees*, 46–47.

7   Suzanne Simard, *Finding the Mother Tree: Discovering the Wisdom of the Forest* (New York: Knopf, 2021), 175–76.

8   "How Do Plants Grow toward the Light? Scientists Explain Mechanism behind Phototropism," Science Daily, May 28, 2013, https://www.sciencedaily.com/releases/2013/05/130528105946.htm.

9   Wohlleben, *The Hidden Life of Trees*, 33.

10   Peter Wohlleben, *The Power of Trees: How Ancient Forests Can Save Us If We Let Them* (Berkeley: Greystone Books, 2021), 72.

11   Katherine May, *Wintering; The Power of Rest and Retreat in Difficult Times* (New York: Riverhead Books, 2020), 69.

12   Eetu Puttonen et al., "Quantification of Overnight Movement of Birch (Betula Pendula) Branches and Foliage with Short Interval Terrestrial Laser Scanning," *Frontiers in Plant Science* 7 (2016), https://www.frontiersin.org/articles/10.3389/fpls.2016.00222.

13   Wohlleben, *The Hidden Life of Trees*, 148–49.

14   Barbara Brown Taylor, *Learning to Walk in the Dark* (New York: Harper Collins, 2014), 129.

15   Doyne Cantrell, *Western Cherokee Nation of Arkansas and Missouri—A History—A Heritage* (lulu.com, 2009), 122–23.

Chapter 7: It's All Connected

1   Suzanne Simard, *Finding the Mother Tree: Discovering the Wisdom of the Forest* (New York: Knopf, 2021), 160–61.

2   Peter Wohlleben, *The Hidden Life of Trees: What They Feel, How They Communicate* (Vancouver: Greystone Books, 2015), 15–17.

3 Wohlleben, *The Hidden Life of Trees*, 16–17.

4 Kristin Ohlson, *Sweet in Tooth and Claw: Stories of Generosity and Cooperation in the Natural World* (Ventura, CA: Patagonia Books, 2022), 34.

5 Wohlleben, *The Hidden Life of Trees*, 53.

6 Simard, *Finding the Mother Tree*, 160–61.

7 Meg Lowman, *The Arbornaut: A Life Discovering the Eighth Continent in the Trees Above Us* (New York: Farrar, Straus & Giroux, 2021), 146.

8 Wohlleben, *The Hidden Life of Trees*, 7.

9 Lowman, *The Arbornaut*, 146.

10 Ben Rawlence, *The Treeline: The Last Forest and the Future of Life on Earth* (New York: St. Martin's Press, 2022), 17.

11 "American Values and Assumptions," University of Portland, accessed March 25, 2024, https://www.up.edu/iss/advising-services/american-values.html.

12 Christina Ianzito, "Former Surgeon General Vivek Murthy on Loneliness," AARP, June 6, 2020, https://www.aarp.org/health/healthy-living/info-2020/vivek-murthy-loneliness.html.

13 Ianzito, "Former Surgeon General."

14 The US Surgeon General's Advisory on the Healing Effects of Social Connection and Community, "Our Epidemic of Loneliness and Isolation" (US Public Health Service, 2023), https://www.hhs.gov/sites/default/files/surgeon-general-social-connection-advisory.pdf.

15 Michael Vincent McGinnis, "Species Loneliness," *The Santa Barbara Independent* (blog), January 14, 2012, https://www.independent.com/2012/01/14/species-loneliness/.

16 Terry Tempest Williams, *An Unspoken Hunger: Stories from the Field* (New York: Vintage Books, 1994), 64.

17 The Center for Spirituality in Nature, "Note from Nature: The Human Creature," July 30, 2019, YouTube video, 3:28, https://youtu.be/hFltlDZaDNc?si=IUGa_6IeO2IAQN58.

18 "Pinyon Jay," Audubon Field Guide, accessed December 19, 2023, https://www.audubon.org/field-guide/bird/pinyon-jay.

19 Douglas W. Tallamy, *The Nature of Oaks: The Rich Ecology of Our Most Essential Native Trees* (Portland, OR: Timber Press, 2021), 77.

20 Douglas W. Tallamy, *Nature's Best Hope: A New Approach to Conservation That Starts in Your Yard* (Portland, OR: Timber Press, Inc., 2019), 137.

21 Tallamy, *Nature's Best Hope*, 144.
22 Ohlson, *Sweet in Tooth and Claw*.
23 Ohlson, *Sweet in Tooth and Claw*, 68–69.
24 "Janine Benyus—Biomimicry, an Operating Manual for Earthlings," The On Being Project, March 23, 2023, https://onbeing.org/programs/janine-benyus-biomimicry-an-operating-manual-for-earthlings/.
25 "Janine Benyus."
26 Nikk Ogasa, "Forests Help Reduce Global Warming in More Ways than One," *Science News*, March 24, 2022, https://www.sciencenews.org/article/forest-trees-reduce-global-warming-climate-cooling-carbon.
27 John W. Reid and Thomas E. Lovejoy, *Ever Green: Saving Big Forests to Save the Planet* (New York: W.W. Norton & Company, 2022), 5.
28 Rawlence, *The Treeline*, 171.
29 Rawlence, *The Treeline*, 177.
30 Tallamy, *The Nature of Oaks*, 51–56.
31 Rawlence, *The Treeline*, 185.
32 Martin Luther King, "Letter from Birmingham Jail," August 1963, https://www.csuchico.edu/iege/_assets/documents/susi-letter-from-birmingham-jail.pdf.

Chapter 8: Holding Loss, Bearing Witness

1 Walter J. Burghardt, "Contemplation: A Long, Loving Look at the Real," *Church* (Winter 1989), 14–17.
2 Martin Laird, *Into the Silent Land: A Guide to the Christian Practice of Contemplation* (New York: Oxford University Press, 2006), 117–21.
3 Joanna Macy, "Working through Environmental Despair," in *Ecopsychology: Restoring the Earth/Healing the Mind*, ed. Theodore Roszak, Mary E. Gomes, and Allen D. Kanner (Berkeley: Counterpoint, 1995), 252.
4 Macy, "Working through Environmental Despair," 253–54.
5 Carolyn Finney, *Black Faces, White Spaces: Reimagining the Relationship of African Americans to the Great Outdoors* (Chapel Hill: University of North Carolina Press, 2014), 117.
6 "The National Memorial for Peace and Justice," Legacy Sites, accessed April 1, 2024, https://legacysites.eji.org/about/memorial/.

7   "The American Chestnut Foundation," The American Chestnut Foundation, accessed January 15, 2024, https://tacf.org/.

8   "The American Chestnut Foundation."

9   Melody Schreiber, "Addressing Climate Change Concerns in Practice," *Monitor on Psychology* 50, no. 2 (March 1, 2021): 30, https://www.apa.org/monitor/2021/03/ce-climate-change.

10 Belden C. Lane, *The Great Conversation: Nature and the Care of the Soul* (New York: Oxford University Press, 2019), 38–39. Italics in the original.

11 John O'Donohue, *Beauty: The Invisible Embrace* (New York: HarperCollins, 2003), 11.

12 John W. Reid and Thomas E. Lovejoy, *Ever Green: Saving Big Forests to Save the Planet* (New York: W. W. Norton & Company, 2022), 16–18.

13 Ian Austen and Vjosa Isai, "Canada's Logging Industry Devours Forests Crucial to Fighting Climate Change," *The New York Times*, January 4, 2024, https://www.nytimes.com/2024/01/04/world/canada/canada-boreal-forest-logging.html.

14 One hectare is equal to 2.47 acres.

15 Richard Schiffman, "Demand for Meat Is Destroying the Amazon. Smarter Choices at the Dinner Table Can Go a Long Way to Help," *Washington Post*, August 1, 2022, https://www.washingtonpost.com/climate-solutions/2022/03/09/amazon-rainforest-deforestation-beef/.

16 Reid and Lovejoy, *Ever Green*, 103–4.

17 Manuela Andreoni, "Why Palm Oil Is Still a Big Problem," *The New York Times*, March 26, 2024, https://www.nytimes.com/2024/03/26/climate/why-palm-oil-is-still-a-big-problem.html.

18 "COP26: Landmark $500 Million Agreement Launched to Protect the DR Congo's Forest," Africa Renewal, November 10, 2021, https://www.un.org/africarenewal/magazine/december-2021/cop26-landmark-500-million-agreement-launched-protect-dr-congo%E2%80%99s-forest.

19 Ben Rawlence, *The Treeline: The Last Forest and the Future of Life on Earth* (New York: St. Martin's Press, 2022), 79–85.

20 Gleb Raygorodetsky, "Indigenous Peoples Defend Earth's Biodiversity—but They're in Danger," *National Geographic*, November 16, 2018, https://www.nationalgeographic.com/environment/article/can-indigenous-land-stewardship-protect-biodiversity-.

21 Enrique Salmon, "Kincentric Ecology: Indigenous Perceptions of the Human-Nature Relationship," *Ecological Society of America* 10, no. 5 (October 2000): 1327–32.

22 Bioneers, "Casey Camp-Horinek—Walking the Red Road—It's Elemental," 2024, https://conference.bioneers.org/casey-camp-horinek-keynote-address/.

23 Raygorodetsky, "Indigenous Peoples Defend Earth's Biodiversity."

24 Osprey Orielle Lake, *The Story Is in Our Bones: How Worldviews and Climate Justice Can Remake a World in Crisis* (Gabriola Island, BC: New Society Publishers, 2024), 75.

25 Lake, *The Story Is in Our Bones*, 164.

26 Lake, *The Story Is in Our Bones*, 75.

27 "Wildfires Kill Unprecedented Numbers of Large Sequoia Trees," National Park Service, accessed January 18, 2024, https://www.nps.gov/articles/000/wildfires-kill-unprecedented-numbers-of-large-sequoia-trees.htm.

28 "Wildfires Kill Unprecedented Numbers of Large Sequoia Trees."

29 Erik Stokstad, "Ancient Redwoods Recover from Fire by Sprouting 1000-Year-Old Buds," *Science*, December 1, 2023, https://www.science.org/content/article/ancient-redwoods-recover-fire-sprouting-1000-year-old-buds.

30 Ashley Jordan, "The Issue with Tissue Fifth Edition" (New York: Natural Resources Defense Council, 2023), https://www.nrdc.org/sites/default/files/2023-09/issue-with-tissue-5th-report.pdf.

Chapter 9: Comfort, Resilience, and Healing

1 Belden C. Lane, *The Great Conversation: Nature and the Care of the Soul* (New York: Oxford University Press, 2019), 6.

2 "Rewild and Recover," Trees for Life, accessed April 5, 2024, https://treesforlife.org.uk/support/volunteer/rewild-and-recover/.

3 Robin Wall Kimmerer, *Braiding Sweetgrass: Indigenous Wisdom, Scientific Knowledge, and the Teachings of Plants* (Minneapolis: Milkweed Editions, 2013), 340.

4 Kingsley Ighobor, "Wangari Maathai, the Woman of Trees, Dies," *United Nations Africa Renewal*, accessed April 4, 2024, https://www.un.org/africarenewal/web-features/wangari-maathai-woman-trees-dies.

5 "The Chestnut Tree," Anne Frank House, accessed April 4, 2024, https://www.annefrank.org/en/anne-frank/front-section/chestnut-tree/.

6 Sharon Gang, "Anne Frank Tree at the Capitol," *The Architect of the Capitol*, July 21, 2014, https://www.aoc.gov/explore-capitol-campus/blog/anne-frank-tree-capitol.

7 Howard Thurman, *With Head and Heart* (San Diego: Harcourt Brace & Company, 1979), 9.

8 Florence Williams, *The Nature Fix: Why Nature Makes Us Happier, Healthier, and More Creative* (New York: W.W. Norton & Company, 2017).

9 Ingrid D. van Iperen, Jolanda Maas, and Peter E. Spronk, "Greenery and Outdoor Facilities to Improve the Wellbeing of Critically Ill Patients, Their Families and Caregivers: Things to Consider," *Intensive Care Medicine* 49, no. 10 (August 23, 2023): 1229–31, https://www.ncbi.nlm.nih.gov/pmc/articles/PMC10556109/.

10 Rahawa Haile, "'Forest Bathing': How Microdosing on Nature Can Help with Stress," *The Atlantic*, June 30, 2017, https://www.theatlantic.com/health/archive/2017/06/forest-bathing/532068/.

11 "Forest Therapy Guide Training," The Association of Nature & Forest Therapy, accessed April 4, 2024, https://www.anft.earth/guide-training/training.

12 Leah Rampy, *Earth & Soul: Reconnecting Amid Climate Chaos* (Chevy Chase, MD: Bold Story Press, 2024), 70–71.

13 Peter Wohlleben, *The Power of Trees: How Ancient Forests Can Save Us If We Let Them* (Berkeley: Greystone Books, 2021), 9.

14 James B. Nardi, *The Hidden Company That Trees Keep: Life from Treetops to Root Tips* (Princeton, NJ: Princeton University Press, 2003), 8.

15 Nardi, *The Hidden Company That Trees Keep*, 7–11.

16 Joelle G. Novey, "How Can I Bear It Alone?" (Tifereth Israel Congregation, Washington, DC, July 22, 2023).

17 I'm indebted to Sam Chase and the Kripalu Center for the idea of "showing up" as an important aspect of resilience.

18 Jack Kornfield, *The Wise Heart: A Guide to the Universal Teachings of Buddhist Psychology* (New York: Bantam Books, 2009), 101–6.

19 Cynthia Bourgeault, *The Wisdom Way of Knowing: Reclaiming an Ancient Tradition to Awaken the Heart* (San Francisco: Jossey-Bass, 2003), 110–11.

20 Cynthia Bourgeault, *The Wisdom Jesus: Transforming Heart and Mind—a New Perspective on Christ and His Message* (Boulder: Shambhala Publications, 2008), 181.

21 Thomas Merton and Kathleen Deignan, *When the Trees Say Nothing: Writings on Nature* (Notre Dame, IN: Sorin Books, 2003), 171.

Chapter 10: Gratitude and Reciprocity

1 OAR US EPA, "Heat Island Effect," Collections and Lists, February 28, 2014, https://www.epa.gov/heatislands.

2 Vittoria Traverso, "The Best Trees to Reduce Air Pollution," May 4, 2020, https://www.bbc.com/future/article/20200504-which-trees-reduce-air-pollution-best.

3 OAR US EPA, "Using Trees and Vegetation to Reduce Heat Islands," Overviews and Factsheets, June 17, 2014, https://www.epa.gov/heatislands/using-trees-and-vegetation-reduce-heat-islands.

4 "Expressing Gratitude to Improve Health," Mayo Clinic Health System, December 6, 2022, https://www.mayoclinichealthsystem.org/hometown-health/speaking-of-health/can-expressing-gratitude-improve-health.

5 "West Virginia Northern Flying Squirrel," Center for Biological Diversity, accessed May 8, 2022, https://www.biologicaldiversity.org/species/mammals/West_Virginia_northern_flying_squirrel/index.html.

6 David George Haskell, *The Forest Unseen: A Year's Watch in Nature* (New York: Penguin Books, 2012), 153.

7 Robin Wall Kimmerer, *Braiding Sweetgrass: Indigenous Wisdom, Scientific Knowledge, and the Teachings of Plants* (Minneapolis: Milkweed Editions, 2013), 285.

8 Kimmerer, *Braiding Sweetgrass*, 289.

9 Kimmerer, *Braiding Sweetgrass*, 290.

10 Cal Flyn, *Islands of Abandonment: Nature Rebounding in the Post-Human Landscape* (New York: Penguin Books, 2022), 101.

11 Peter Wohlleben, *The Power of Trees: How Ancient Forests Can Save Us If We Let Them* (Berkeley: Greystone Books, 2021), 83.

12 Osprey Orielle Lake, *The Story Is in Our Bones: How World-views and Climate Justice Can Remake a World in Crisis* (Gabriola Island, BC: New Society Publishers, 2024), 159.

13 Lake, *The Story Is in Our Bones*, 164.

14 John W. Reid and Thomas E. Lovejoy, *Ever Green: Saving Big Forests to Save the Planet* (New York: W. W. Norton & Company, 2022), 245–46.

15 Reid and Lovejoy, *Ever Green*, 246–47.

16 "Lawns to Life! Initiative," SOS: Save Our Soil, accessed February 18, 2024, https://www.saveoursoilwv.com/lawns-to-life1.html.

17 Douglas W. Tallamy, *Nature's Best Hope: A New Approach to Conservation That Starts in Your Yard* (Portland, OR: Timber Press, Inc., 2019), 62.

18 Kimmerer, *Braiding Sweetgrass*, 290.

Chapter 11: Renewal and Hope

1 "1988 Fires," National Park Service, accessed April 6, 2024, https://www.nps.gov/yell/learn/nature/1988-fires.htm.

2 David A. Perry, Ram Oren, and Stephen C. Hart, *Forest Ecosystems* (Baltimore: Johns Hopkins University Press, 2008), 121.

3 Perry, Oren, and Hart, *Forest Ecosystems*, 438.

4 Joanna Macy and Chris Johnstone, *Active Hope: How to Face the Mess We're in without Going Crazy* (Novato, CA: New World Library), 1.

5 Rebecca Solnit, *Hope in the Dark: Untold Histories, Wild Possibilities* (Chicago: Haymarket Books, 2016), xiv.

6 Macy and Johnstone, *Active Hope*, 141.

7 Peter Wohlleben, *The Power of Trees: How Ancient Forests Can Save Us If We Let Them* (Berkeley: Greystone Books, 2021), 241.

SELECTED BIBLIOGRAPHY

Beresford-Kroeger, Diana. *To Speak for the Trees: My Life's Journey from Ancient Celtic Wisdom to a Healing Vision of the Forest.* Toronto: Random House, 2019.

Boss, Gayle. *All Creation Waits: The Advent Mystery of New Beginnings.* Brewster, MA: Paraclete Press, 2016.

Bourgeault, Cynthia. *The Heart of Centering Prayer: Nondual Christianity in Theory and Practice.* Boulder: Shambala Publications, 2016.

———. *The Wisdom Jesus: Transforming Heart and Mind—a New Perspective on Christ and His Message.* Boulder: Shambhala Publications, 2008.

———. *The Wisdom Way of Knowing: Reclaiming an Ancient Tradition to Awaken the Heart.* San Francisco: Jossey-Bass, 2003.

Brady, Nyle C., and Ray R. Weil. *The Nature and Properties of Soils.* Uttar Pradesh, India: Pearson, 2014.

Brown Taylor, Barbara. *Learning to Walk in the Dark.* New York: Harper Collins, 2014.

Buhner, Stephen Harrod. *Earth Grief: The Journey into and through Ecological Loss.* Boulder: Raven Press, 2022.

———. *The Secret Teachings of Plants: The Intelligence of the Heart in the Direct Perception of Nature.* Rochester, VT: Bear & Company, 2004.

Burnie, David. *Tree: Discover the World of Trees—from Tiny Saplings to Forest Giants.* London: DK Publishing, 2005.

Chase, Steven. *Nature as Spiritual Practice.* Grand Rapids: William B. Eerdmans Publishing, 2011.

Chödrön, Pema. *When Things Fall Apart: Heart Advice for Difficult Times*. Boulder: Shambhala Publications, 2016.

Christie, Douglas E. *The Blue Sapphire of the Mind: Notes for a Contemplative Ecology*. New York: Oxford University Press, 2013.

Clifford, M. Amos. *Your Guide to Forest Bathing: Experience the Healing Power of Nature*. Newburyport, MA: Conari Press, 2018.

Dungy, Camille T. *Soil: The Story of a Black Mother's Garden*. New York: Simon & Schuster, 2023.

Finney, Carolyn. *Black Faces, White Spaces: Reimaging the Relationship of African Americans to the Great Outdoors*. Chapel Hill: University of North Carolina Press, 2014.

Flyn, Cal. *Islands of Abandonment: Nature Rebounding in the Post-Human Landscape*. New York: Penguin Books, 2021.

Gooley, Tristan. *How to Read a Tree: Clues and Patterns from Bark to Leaves: Learn to Navigate by Branches, Locate Water with a Leaf, and Unlock Other Secrets in Trees*. New York: The Experiment, 2023.

Hageneder, Fred. *The Living Wisdom of Trees: A Guide to the Natural History, Symbolism and Healing Power of Trees*. London: Watkins, 2020.

———. *The Meaning of Trees: Botany, History, Healing, Lore*. San Francisco: Chronicle Books, 2005.

Haskell, David George. *The Forest Unseen: A Year's Watch in Nature*. New York: Viking, 2012.

———. *The Songs of Trees; Stories from Nature's Great Connectors*. New York: Viking, 2017.

Haupt, Lyanda Lynn. *Rooted: Life at the Crossroads of Science, Nature, and Spirit*. New York: Little, Brown Spark, 2011.

Heinrich, Bernd. *The Trees in My Forest*. New York: Cliff Street Books, 1997.

Hesse, Hermann. *Wandering*. Translated by James Wright. New York: Farrar, Straus & Giroux, 1972.

Hiss, Tony. *Rescuing the Planet: Protecting Half the Land to Heal the Earth*. New York: Vintage Books, 2021.

Johnson, James Weldon. *God's Trombones: Seven Negro Sermons in Verse*. New York: Penguin Books, 2008.

Kaza, Stephanie. *The Attentive Heart: Conversations with Trees*. Boston: Shambhala Publications, 1996.

Keltner, Dacher. *Awe: The New Science of Everyday Wonder and How It Can Transform Your Life*. New York: Penguin Press, 2023.

Kimmerer, Robin Wall. *Braiding Sweetgrass: Indigenous Wisdom, Scientific Knowledge, and the Teachings of Plants.* Minneapolis: Milkweed Editions, 2013.

Kornfield, Jack. *The Wise Heart: A Guide to the Universal Teachings of Buddhist Psychology.* New York: Bantam Books, 2009.

Laird, Martin. *Into the Silent Land: A Guide to the Christian Practice of Contemplation.* New York: Oxford University Press, 2006.

Lane, Belden C. *The Great Conversation: Nature and the Care of the Soul.* New York: Oxford University Press, 2019.

Levertov, Denise. *Breathing the Water.* New York: New Directions Publishing, 1987.

Logan, William Bryant. *Dirt: The Ecstatic Skin of the Earth.* W.W. Norton & Company, 1995.

Lowman, Meg. *The Arbornaut: A Life Discovering the Eighth Continent in the Trees above Us.* New York: Farrar, Straus & Giroux, 2021.

Macy, Joanna. "Working through Environmental Despair." In *Ecopsychology: Restoring the Earth/Healing the Mind,* edited by Theordore Roszak, Mary E. Gomes, and Allen D. Kanner, 240–59. Berkeley: Counterpoint, 1995.

Macy, Joanna, and Chris Johnstone. *Active Hope: How to Face the Mess We're in without Going Crazy.* Novato, CA: New World Library, 2012.

Martin, Laura. *Breaking Into Light.* Washington, DC: Opus Self-Publishing Services, 2023.

Matthews, Westina, Margaret Benefiel, and Jackson Droney, eds. *Soul Food: Nourishing Essays on Contemplative Living and Leadership.* New York: Church Publishing, 2023.

May, Katherine. *Wintering: The Power of Rest and Retreat in Difficult Times.* New York: Riverhead Books, 2020.

Merton, Thomas, and Kathleen Deignan. *When the Trees Say Nothing: Writings on Nature.* Notre Dame, IN: Sorin Books, 2003.

Nardi, James B. *The Hidden Company That Trees Keep: Life from Treetops to Root Tips.* Princeton, NJ: Princeton University Press, 2003.

O'Donohue, John. *Beauty: The Invisible Embrace.* New York: HarperCollins, 2003.

Ohlson, Kristin. *Sweet in Tooth and Claw: Stories of Generosity and Cooperation in the Natural World.* Ventura, CA: Patagonia Books, 2022.

Oliver, Mary. *Devotions: The Selected Poems of Mary Oliver.* New York: Penguin Books, 2017.

Perry, David A., Ram Oren, and Stephen C. Hart. *Forest Ecosystems.* Baltimore: Johns Hopkins University Press, 2008.

Plotkin, Bill. "Inscendence: The Key to the Great Work of Our Time (A Soulcentric View of Thomas Berry's Work)." In *Dreamer of the Earth: The Spiritual Ecology of the Father of Environmentalism,* edited by Ervin Laszlo and Allan Combs, 42–71. Rochester, VT: Inner Traditions, 2011.

Rampy, Leah. *Earth & Soul: Reconnecting Amid Climate Chaos.* Chevy Chase, MD: Bold Story Press, 2024.

Rawlence, Ben. *The Treeline: The Last Forest and the Future of Life on Earth.* New York: St. Martin's Press, 2022.

Reid, John W., and Thomas E. Lovejoy. *Ever Green: Saving Big Forests to Save the Planet.* New York: W.W. Norton & Company, 2022.

Riley, Cole Arthur. *This Here Flesh: Spirituality, Liberation, and the Stories That Make Us.* New York: Convergent, 2022.

Roszak, Theodore, ed. *Ecopsychology: Restoring the Earth/Healing the Mind.* Berkeley: Counterpoint, 1995.

Sanders, Scott. *The Way of Imagination: Essays.* New York: Catapult, 2020.

Sheldrake, Merlin. *Entangled Life: How Fungi Make Our Worlds, Change Our Minds, & Shape Our Futures.* New York: Random House, 2020.

Simard, Suzanne. *Finding the Mother Tree: Discovering the Wisdom of the Forest.* New York: Knopf, 2021.

Solnit, Rebecca. *Hope in the Dark: Untold Histories, Wild Possibilities.* Chicago: Haymarket Books, 2016.

Tallamy, Douglas W. *The Nature of Oaks: The Rich Ecology of Our Most Essential Native Trees.* Portland, OR: Timber Press, 2021.

———. *Nature's Best Hope: A New Approach to Conservation That Starts in Your Backyard.* Portland, OR: Timber Press, 2019.

Taylor, Bron. *Dark Green Religion: Nature Spirituality and the Planetary Future.* Oakland: University of California Press, 2010.

Thurman, Howard. *Deep Is the Hunger: Meditations for Apostles of Sensitiveness.* Richmond, IN: Friends United Press, 2000.

———. *With Head and Heart.* San Diego: Harcourt Brace & Company, 1979.

Tillich, Paul. *Systematic Theology.* Vol. 1. Chicago: University of Chicago Press, 1951.

Vorderbruggen, Joan. *Wild Calm: Finding Mindfulness in Forest Bathing.* New York: St. Martin's Press, 2019.

Wessels, Tom. *Forest Forensics: A Field Guide to Reading the Forested Landscape*. Woodstock, VT: Countryman Press, 2010.

Williams, Florence. *The Nature Fix: Why Nature Makes Us Happier, Healthier, and More Creative*. New York: W.W. Norton & Company, 2017.

Wohlleben, Peter. *The Hidden Life of Trees: What They Feel, How They Communicate*. Vancouver: Greystone Books, 2016.

———. *The Power of Trees: How Ancient Forests Can Save Us If We Let Them*. Berkeley: Greystone Books, 2021.

Wood, Douglas. *Fawn Island*. Minneapolis: University of Minnesota Press, 2001.

INDEX